UNION INTERNATIONALE DES SCIENCES PRÉHISTORIQUES ET PROTOHISTORIQUES
INTERNATIONAL UNION FOR PREHISTORIC AND PROTOHISTORIC SCIENCES

PROCEEDINGS OF THE XV WORLD CONGRESS (LISBON, 4-9 SEPTEMBER 2006)
ACTES DU XV CONGRÈS MONDIAL (LISBONNE, 4-9 SEPTEMBRE 2006)

Series Editor: Luiz Oosterbeek

VOL. 29

2006
lisboa
uispp
XVcongresso

Session WS20

Rock Art Data Base

New methods and guidelines in archiving and cataloguing

Base de données en art rupestre

Nouvelles méthodes et lignes guide en archivage et catalogage

Edited by

Raffaella Poggiani-Keller, George Dimitriadis,
Fernando Coimbra, Carlo Liborio,
Maria Giuseppina Ruggiero

BAR International Series 1996
2009

Published in 2016 by
BAR Publishing, Oxford

BAR International Series 1996

Proceedings of the XV World Congress of the International Union for Prehistoric and Protohistoric Sciences / Actes du XV Congrès Mondial de l'Union Internationale des Sciences Préhistoriques et Protohistoriques
Rock Art Data Base / Base de données en art rupestre

ISBN 978 1 4073 0530 1

Outgoing President: Vítor Oliveira Jorge; Outgoing Secretary General: Jean Bourgeois
Congress Secretary General: Luiz Oosterbeek (Series Editor)
Incoming President: Pedro Ignacio Shmitz
Incoming Secretary General: Luiz Oosterbeek
Volume Editors: Raffaella Poggiani-Keller, George Dimitriadis, Fernando Coimbra, Carlo Liborio, Maria Giuseppina Ruggiero

Contacts : Secretary of U.I.S.P.P. – International Union for Prehistoric and Protohistoric Sciences
Instituto Politécnico de Tomar, Av. Dr. Cândido Madureira 13, 2300 TOMAR
Email: uispp@ipt.pt www.uispp.ipt.pt

BAR Publishing is the trading name of British Archaeological Reports (Oxford) Ltd. British Archaeological Reports was first incorporated in 1974 to publish the BAR Series, International and British. In 1992 Hadrian Books Ltd became part of the BAR group. This volume was originally published by Archaeopress in conjunction with British Archaeological Reports (Oxford) Ltd / Hadrian Books Ltd, the Series principal publisher, in 2009. This present volume is published by BAR Publishing, 2016.

Printed in England

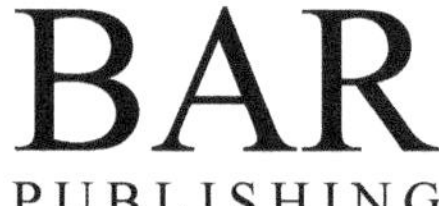

BAR titles are available from:

BAR Publishing
122 Banbury Rd, Oxford, OX2 7BP, UK
EMAIL info@barpublishing.com
PHONE +44 (0)1865 310431
FAX +44 (0)1865 316916
www.barpublishing.com

TABLE OF CONTENTS

LIST OF FIGURES

LIST OF TABLES

INTRODUCTION

In archaeology, as in many other fields, information technology has acquired a fundamental role in the archiving and management of the large quantity of information gathered during excavation, or the study of a site, monument or class of finds.

Research into rock art, a patrimony of worldwide occurrence, requires on the part of archaeologists (and others) the capacity to communicate knowledge, methods and experience, to create a common base for debate open to all and for the elaboration of agreed procedures. It was with these aims in mind that we organized this workshop, which was coordinated by a number of institutions and organizations – the Italian Ministry for Cultural Heritage and Activities and Lombardy Archaeological Heritage Superintendency, the Hellenic Rock Art Centre of Philippi (Greece), the University of Salamanca (Spain) and the Archaeological Cooperative Society (Milan, Italy) – which collaborated in the design of a uniform recording system and intend to work together in the future on similar projects. The goal of developing standardized procedures for the recording and conservation of rock engravings is also pursued by the Paris UNESCO headquarters, which in May 2006 invited the Lombardy Superintendency for Archaeological Heritage to present the IRWEB cataloguing and monitoring system at the "1ère réunion d'experts en Art rupestre dans les Caraïbes et Liste du patrimoine mondial de l'UNESCO a Basse Terre (Guadeloupe)" 3rd – 6th May 2006, coordinated by Nuria Sanz, which aimed at the adoption of uniform methods in the numerous UNESCO rock art sites. The UISPP conference in September 2006 was thus a second opportunity to compare ideas and seek to develop a standardized system, or family of intercommunicating systems, based on information technology.

Contributions in the field of computerized inventories presented at Workshop 20 included methods of information recording and applications (database) developed in South America (Colombia) and Europe; the latter category comprised joint European projects and a system created in Italy. Naturally, for various reasons, the projects presented at the UISPP XV Congress constituted only a part of those that are actually in use at present on rock art sites throughout the world, but it seems useful nevertheless to comment on the majority tendencies which emerged.

It was immediately clear from the diverse applications illustrated and papers presented that much attention is being given (as well as to the "traditional" themes of iconography, artistic techniques etc.) to the theme of conservation, seen today as fundamentally important for the preservation of the world's rich heritage of rock art for future generations. Another important aspect which emerged was the necessity to render accessible information which in many cases was gathered some time ago and today forms a historical archive, adapting it to technological advances and maintaining pace with future developments.

The GIPRI team has been working since the 1970s on methods for recording Colombian rock art (Guillermo Muñoz, Judith Trujillo, *Inventarios gráficos y geográficos: un proyecto de registro y conservación del arte rupestre en Colombia*). The system has undergone several phases of development (1996-98, 2000-2005) to permit adaptation to the continued evolution in programmes for digital manipulation and GIS (Geographical Systems of Information). The initial use of a Cartesian base for recording information facilitated the process of transferral to new technologies; the most recent version is a GIS which combines drawn and photographic records in a form which is useful for the conservation and management of rock art sites.

IRWEB is the cataloguing system developed in Italy by the Lombardy Archaeological Superintendency (Raffaella Poggiani Keller, Carlo Liborio, Maria Giuseppina Ruggiero, *The rock art database by the Ministry of Cultural Heritage and Activities-Soprintendenza for Archaeological Heritage of Lombardia: from IR project to IRWEB*) which is responsible for one of the richest and best known areas of rock art: the Camonica Valley, in the World Heritage List since 1979. Here too, the primary aim was to record the preservation state of the engraved rocks. The project was begun in 1989 and took on its modern form in 1997, with continual adaptation to developments in software, an instrument for the management of technical, scientific and administrative aspects, with a stress on monitoring the rocks' state of preservation.

The programme is based on the Cultural Heritage Risk Map that was drawn up after many years' work during the 1990s by the Central Institute for Conservation's Central Institute for Cataloguing and Records and tested in Valle Camonica and Valtellina in 1997 (Angela Maria Ferroni, *The Risk Map and rock engravings*). On that occasion it was discovered that biological, physical and mechanical damage are strictly correlated with human activity and that routine conservation of the rocks is an essential part of a medium and long term planning strategy for preservation treatment, with its continually rising costs.

The theme of conservation of engraved rocks, with reference to the rock art of eastern Macedonia (Greece), was also addressed by the "Hellenic Rock Art Documentation Project" (HRAD), developed at HERAC, the Hellenic Rock Art Centre, Philippi (George Dimitriadis, Fernando Coimbra, Carmelo Prestipino, *Philippi rock art. Guidelines for a methodological recovery and preventive action*). Data related to preservation state were recorded during a survey of the area, followed by an analysis of the treatment needed to conserve the rock surfaces for future study and the putting into practice of this work in the field. In this case the rocks were covered with special membranes and a sand mixture designed to reduce humidity, temperature differences and exposure to sunlight, factors implicated in the growth of lichens and plants and erosion by exfoliation.

The Europreart database (Dario Seglie, *The Europreart project – past signs and present memories. European Prehistoric Art: inventory, contextualisation, preservation and accessibility*), in addition to topographic and archaeological information, also takes into consideration aspects concerning conservation. In this case the project is the result of an attempt at a Europe-wide, not just national, level to create a data bank regarding all manifestations of rock art throughout the continent. The system uses Microsoft Access, and has the merit of having devised a common vocabulary, in English, covering the needs and peculiarities of various geographical and cultural areas and of having worked in close collaboration with the most important institutions responsible at an international level for rock art and the tutelage of cultural heritage (IFRAO, UNESCO and UISPP).

Since the need to develop a common vocabulary for an area as large as Europe has inevitably led to an agreed selection of data collection fields on the basis of a sort of lowest common denominator, one would hope for a future collaboration between Europreart and the nationally-based projects, which could supply greater detail on specific themes.

The paper "Web sites and Intellectual Property Rights (IPR)" analyses this delicate and topical subject that becomes ever more relevant as the number of on-line databases available increases. In recent years the "Web world" has been subjected to rules and regulations almost as much as the "analogical world" and thus actions taken through the Web which threaten individual or collective rights are equally actionable and punishable (Giuliana De Francesco, *Web sites and Intellectual Property Rights*).[1]

In a world which is ever more dependent on information technology and increasingly interconnected due to the spread of the Internet, data management and data security (involving texts and images, often unpublished) have become important problems which organizations and institutions have to face. These topics have been addressed during successive updates of the IRWEB system, which since 2003 has been accessible via Internet; in particular, "security levels, data validation and publication procedures, grouped access to sets of data" (Daniele Vitali, Luca Megale, *The digital cataloguing of rock art on the Web: server-client architecture and on-line partnership*). Also, since access to IRWEB information occurs at different levels with on-line registration of personal details, the right to privacy and the matter of accessibility were discussed. In Italy these are regulated by D. Lgs. N° 196, 30th June 2003 and Law N° 4, 9th January 2004, respectively.

Another question considered during the development of IRWEB was that of the use of images which are the property of organizations but which, since they are frequently present in on-line archives, can be downloaded from the Web for personal motives, use in teaching etc. It is necessary to protect images of cultural heritage against commercial exploitation and to safeguard intellectual property rights. IRWEB images are protected by "advanced watermarking techniques in conjunction with a Digital Rights Management system based on strong digital signatures, in order to enable web archives to publish protected images and have a legal proof of ownership of them" (Daniele Vitali, Luca Megale, *Digital rights management for archived pictures in web contexts*).

Lastly, the theme of modern technology was continued by a paper describing a recent experiment in the use of a laser scanner conducted in Valle Camonica on a rock discovered in 2005 in Bedolina locality, Capo di Ponte, Province of Brescia, Italy (Emilio Colombo Zefinetti, Piergiorgio Peverelli, *New technology for rock art documentation by the Soprintendenza for Archaeological Heritage of Lombardia: laser scanner in Valle Camonica-Italy*). A laser scanner allows the creation of an accurate three-dimensional image of the rock surface, useful both for the purposes of study and conservation monitoring. Engraved rocks rarely have flat surfaces which may easily be drawn by archaeologists. Laser scanner technology has been employed in the USA, UK and Sweden since the 1990s, and has reached high levels of definition and precision with falling costs, thanks to developments in the instruments and relevant software. Another method that has been used for recording rock surfaces in the IRWEB project and "Hellenic Rock Art Documentation Project" is photogrammetry.

The picture which clearly emerges is that rock art studies is a branch of archaeology which is particularly dynamic and open to the innovations of information technology. Our aim for the future must be that of defining common technical standards and guidelines for digital archives.

[1] For further information concerning data protection and intellectual property rights with regard to the accessibility of cultural heritage, see the site of MINERVA, MInisterial NEtwoRk for Valorising Activities in digitisation, a European project started in 2002. This was defined as "a network of Member States' Ministries to discuss, correlate and harmonise activities carried out in digitisation of cultural and scientific content for creating an agreed European common platform, recommendations and guidelines about digitisation, metadata, long-term accessibility and preservation"; www.minervaeurope.org.

WS20 was coordinated by:
Maria Giuseppina Ruggiero, Archaeological Cooperative Society (Italy)
Raffaella Poggiani Keller, Lombardy Superintendency for Archaeological Heritage (Italy)
Carlo Liborio, Archaeological Cooperative Society (Italy)
George Dimitriadis, HERAC (Hellenic Rock Art Centre, Greece)
Fernando Coimbra, USAL (University of Salamanca, Spain)

Thanks to Jim Bishop and Silvia Dondi, who collaborated in the translation in English and French.

THE RISK MAP AND ROCK ENGRAVINGS

Angela Maria FERRONI
Ministero per i Beni e le Attività Culturali, Dipartimento per la Ricerca, l'Innovazione e l'Organizzazione, Ufficio Patrimonio Mondiale Unesco, Via del Collegio Romano, 27, 00186 Roma, ITALY
E-mail: aferroni@beniculturali.it

***Abstract**: In 1997 the Central Institute for Restoration (ICR) of the Italian Ministry for Cultural Heritage and Activities performed in the framework of the Risk Map of Cultural Heritage some experimental cataloguing on rocks engraved in Valle Camonica and in Valtellina. This initiative, targeted at analysing conservative aspects, has highlighted how the biological, physical and mechanical degradation of rocks are closely related to the anthropic one (trampling, vandalism and rock cleaning performed by non specialist personnel). The analysis disclosed that rocks in better states of conservation are doubtless those situated in protected areas, where ordinary maintenance is constantly performed. Hence the crucial relevance of accurate and regular maintenance, failing which even the most rigorous restoration works run the risk of loosing effectiveness.*
***Keywords**: Rock art, risk map, Valle Camonica, Valtellina, conservative aspects*

***Résumé**: En 1997 l'Institut central pour la restauration (ICR) et l'Institut central pour le catalogage et la documentation (ICCD) du Ministère italien pour le patrimoine culturel, dans le cadre de la réalisation d'une Carte des risques du patrimoine culturel italien, ont effectué un catalogage expérimental des roches gravées de la Valle Camonica et de la Valtellina. Cette initiative était visée à l'analyse de l'état de conservation des gravures et a mis en évidence que la dégradation biologique, physique et mécanique des roches est étroitement liée aux aspects anthropiques (piétinement, vandalisme et nettoyage effectué par personnel non spécialisé). L'étude a démontré que les roches en meilleur état sont certainement celles qui se trouvent à l'intérieur des zones protégées et sont l'objet de travaux d'entretien réguliers. On en déduit l'importance cruciale de travaux d'entretien effectués régulièrement et soigneusement car, autrement, même la restauration la plus rigoureuse risque de perdre en efficacité.*
***Mots cles**: Art rupestre, carte des risques, Valle Camonica, Valtellina, aspects de la conservation*

In 1997, within the framework of the *Risk Map of the Italian Cultural Heritage,* the Istituto Centrale del Restauro di Roma-ICR (Rome's Central Institute for Restoration) of the Italian Ministry for Cultural Heritage and Activities carried out experimental cataloguing of engraved rocks situated in Valle Camonica and in Valtellina.

The project known as "*Risk Map of Cultural Heritage*", was implemented in 1990 and is the result of thirty years of studies and research accomplished by ICR in the field of conservation and restoration. The project was aimed at identifying the level of risk endangering cultural heritage on Italian territory, and focussed particularly on the need to plan cultural heritage conservation through prevention of damage.

The ICR had implemented a pilot plan (AA.VV. 1976) as far back as 1975 with Giovanni Urbani and had thus achieved a more specific definition of "preventive restoration", understood as the removal of works of art from environmental conditions that might threaten their conservation. This subject had already been developed by Cesare Brandi in the Sixties (Brandi 1956, pp. 87-92. Urbani 1973, p. 5 sgg.).

The main factors causing deterioration of the cultural heritage were examined in the course of a first feasibility plan, developed in 1987 as part of the programme "Memorabilia: il futuro della memoria" (Baldi; Cordaro; Melucco Vaccaro 1987); these studies resulted in preliminary charts highlighting the territory's seismic classification, dynamics of demographic density and pollution indexes, estimated on the basis of pollutant emissions of industrial plants, etc. However, these first charts were, basically, an approximation because they suffered from a significant simplification of all the data and, more importantly, they lacked an element that is essential for risk evaluation: an effective knowledge of the cultural heritage's vulnerability (Baldi 1992, pp. 8-13). The project *Risk Map,* therefore, corrected and completed these first experiences in the light of an increasingly specific knowledge of deterioration phenomena and of the properties that need to be protected (Baldi 1997, p. 9 sgg).

The idea at the basis of the *Risk Map* is to identify systems and procedures allowing an effective planning of conservation and restoration treatment to be carried out on architectonic, archaeological, historical and artistic properties, according to their respective state of conservation and to the aggressiveness of their environment; "planning" is intended as the possibility to obtain all the information necessary to be able to foresee and decide beforehand all the actions that are more urgent, the delay within which they need to be taken and the costs. The philosophy of periodic monitoring and preventive actions applied to cultural heritage is meant to provide the authorities responsible for cultural heritage protection with an effective instrument to support scientific and administrative activities, an instrument that may favour the "supervision" of the state of conservation

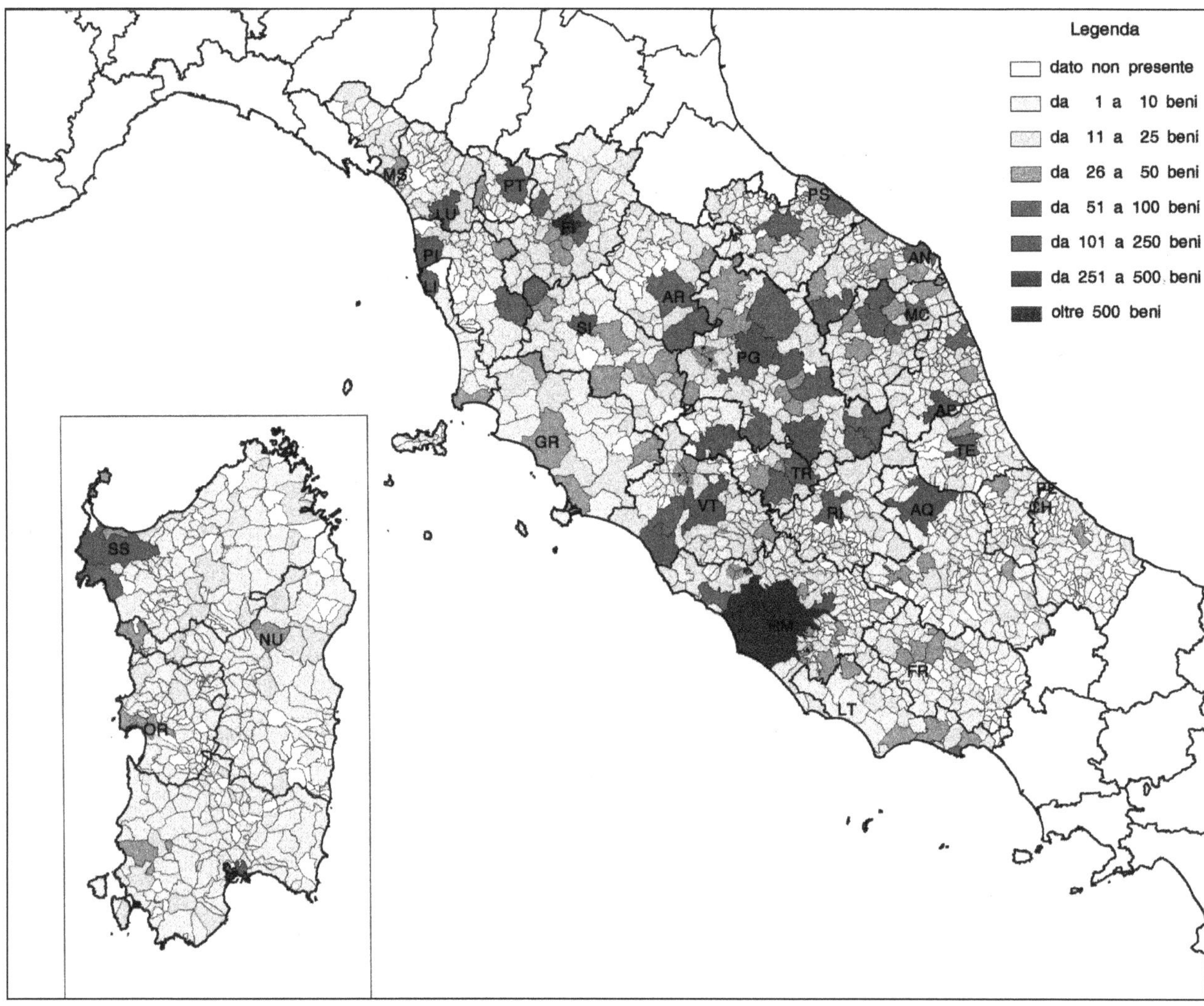

Fig. 1.1. Map of components and distribution of cultural heritage in Central Italy, carried out using as data source TCI Guides of Italy and Laterza archaeological guides

of the properties and, at the same time, allow a better coordination of conservation and restoration activities.

Risk is the possibility that an undesired event may damage something that is considered as having cultural heritage value. Obviously, risk is correlated to two different aspects, dangerousness and vulnerability, where dangerousness is the presence or likelihood that damaging events may occur, what is referred to as factors of territorial danger, and vulnerability is the extent to which a property is prone to damage. The Risk Map is, therefore, a selection of thematic data systematically correlated so as to identify specific causal relationships between the cultural property, its state of conservation, and the factors of territorial danger that bring about its deterioration. These data are collected, processed and managed in a vast alphanumeric and cartographic data bank.

The Risk Map's Geographical Information System (GIS) is updatable and interactive; it covers the national territory as a whole and manages data referred to physical, chemical and social phenomena involved in the deterioration process, as well as data on the state of conservation of single properties. Thanks to this system it is possible to determine specific danger "indices" referred to the distribution of properties and the distribution of danger phenomena over the whole territory; said indices are visible on computerized thematic maps that can be superimposed to provide a first estimate of risk on the territory.

For example, if we overlay the cultural heritage distribution map – which shows quantity and typology of architectonical and archaeological assets derived from a bibliographic survey[1] – and the static-structural danger

[1] Since the Italian heritage was not catalogued, bibliographic data were taken from the Touring Club Guides (Guide d'Italia del Touring Club Italiano) and from the Laterza Archaeological Guides (Guide Archeologiche Laterza). The assets taken into consideration were subdivided into three main categories: archaeological assets, architectural assets, containers of works of art; said classification followed standards and methods used by ICCD; specific information necessary to establish the nature and typology of the assets were also collected: function, location, chronology, present use, tourist value; data

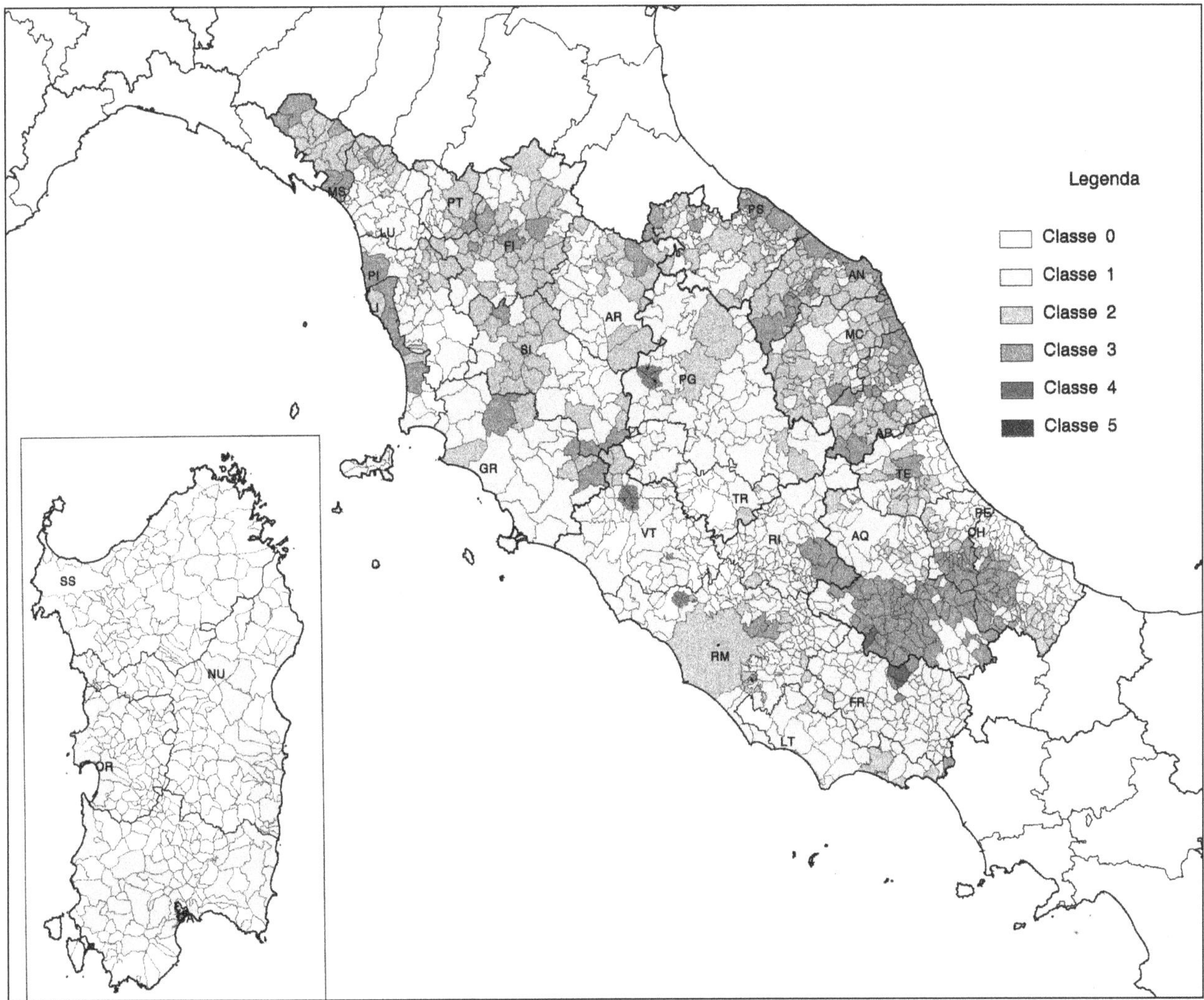

Fig. 1.2. Summary map of static-structural danger, for Central Italy, carried out combining the six specific indicators (due to earthquake activity, landslides and slips, coastal dynamics, flooding, volcanic activity, avalanches)

map – which takes into consideration natural phenomena having a more or less direct incidence on the structural stability of a building, such as earthquakes, landslides and slips, floods, coastal dynamics, avalanches, volcanic activities[2] – we may observe the relation between areas having high static-structural danger and areas in which the presence of monuments is higher. But we may also further increase the degree of specificity of the research and combine static-structural danger maps with maps showing the monuments that are particularly affected by this type of danger, i.e. slender structures such as towers or campaniles. Or again, we may cross data on the presence of atmospheric pollutants shown on the environmental air danger maps – which take into consideration climatic agents (minimum and maximum temperatures, humidity, rainfall, wind direction and intensity) and air pollution factors (estimated emission levels in the municipality of sulphur dioxide, nitrogen monoxide and oxide, estimated mean values of acid rain, particulate concentration)[3] – with data on the distribution of assets that are attacked and damaged by such pollutants, in particular stone monuments and engraved rocks.

The anthropic danger phenomenon, which is more difficult to define and was not, at the time of the studies,

on the possible connection to urban planning contexts or to architectural complexes and on works of art contained were also collected. Bonifica S.p.A. 1996, pp. 11-62; Accardo 2000, pp. 34-45.

[2] Collected data for each phenomenon were processed through the definition of simple algorithms which, on the basis of the presence or absence of the phenomenon, and of its extent and intensity, allow the attribution of a figure known as "**danger index**" to be assigned to each single municipality. A different importance was then assigned to each index in order to elaborate the hierarchy of the various phenomena, with respect to their assumed effect on the cultural assets, and so calculate summarized indices and plot the summarized of static-structural danger maps. Bonifica S.p.A. 1996, pp. 63-98.

[3] A considerable standardization of the data allowed the elaboration of air-environment danger maps and to calculate mathematical models describing the deterioration processes, taking into consideration collected data and a vast number of different factors that also concur in alteration phenomena, in particular structural characteristics and porosity of materials used. An **erosion index** was established (to quantify loss of material of the exposed surfaces caused by meteorological and climatic factors combined to pollution factors), also a **blackening index** and a **physical stress index**. Bonifica S.p.A. 1996, pp. 99-137.

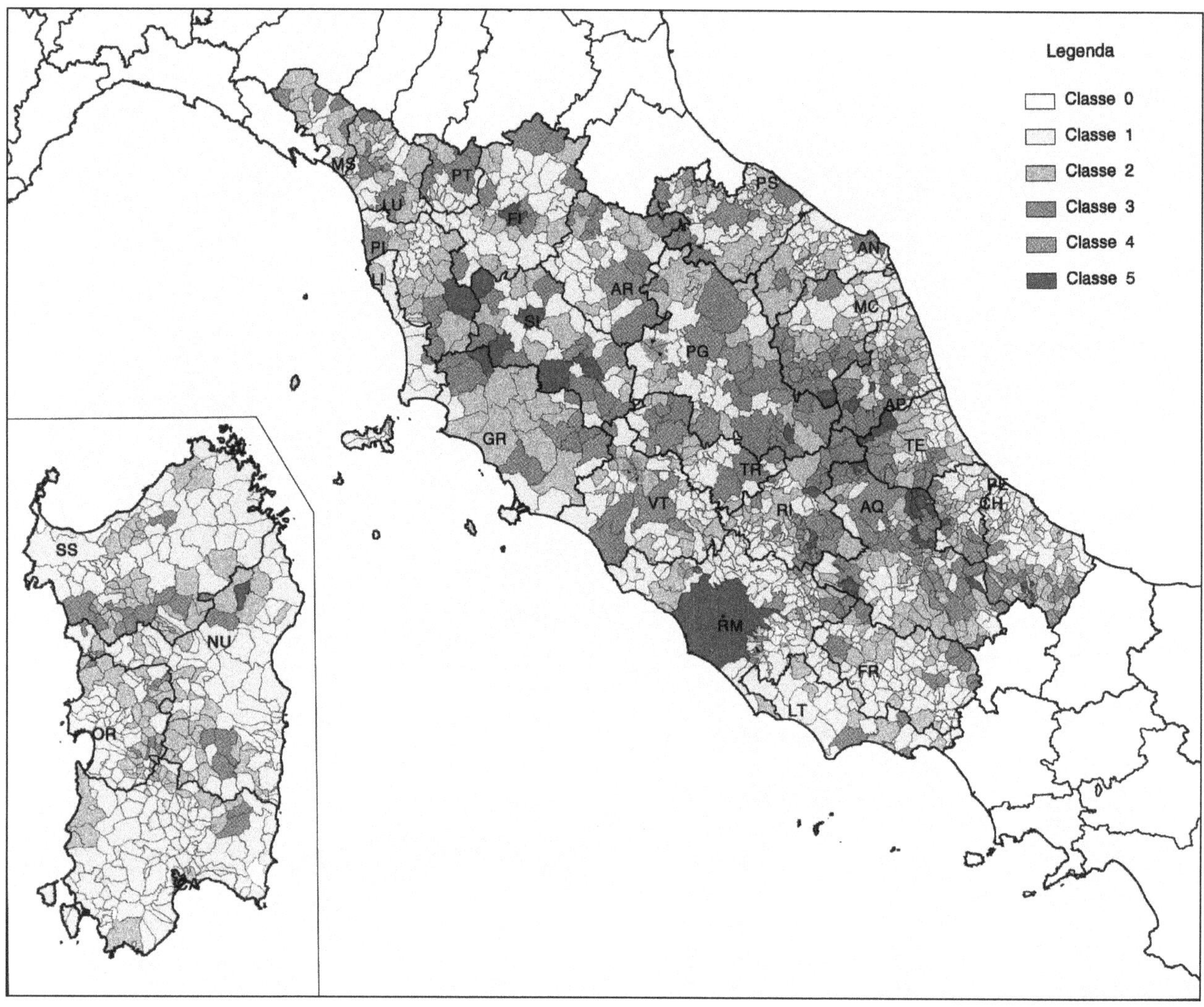

Fig. 1.3. Summary map of danger due to anthropic factors (depopulation/population concentration, tourism, theft) for Central Italy

supported by research and theoretical processing, is brought under three headings: liability to theft; tourism pressure and dynamics of demographic density, for which statistical data were processed and maps produced (Bonifica S.p.A. 1996, pp. 139-173).

While work on the identification of danger indices and elaboration of thematic maps was in progress, a vast-ranging survey on the state of conservation of hundreds of architectonic and archaeological monuments was also carried out in four sample areas.[4] As mentioned earlier, risk is a function of two different aspects, dangerousness and vulnerability. The basic assumption of the Risk Map is that it is possible to measure each single aspect of risk, including vulnerability, which may be considered a latent dimension, and is approximately measurable through different aspects of deterioration: the more a property is deteriorated, the more it is vulnerable to danger factors present in its environment. By associating the vulnerability to the territorial danger indices, a specific calculation procedure allows to determine the "individual risk" of each single monument.

Appropriate data forms were drawn up, following standard cataloguing instruments in use in ICCD (Italian Central Institute for Catalogue and Documentation), to identify the state of conservation of monuments, archaeological areas, decorations and works having artistic and historical value. These forms represent a low cost method to evaluate the extent (as a percentage of the property under examination) and the seriousness and urgency (as the acceleration of the phenomenon expressed with different degrees) of damages observed; they also allow an evaluation of the management conditions and of the monument's urban surroundings (Ferroni, Bianchi 1997, p. 27 sgg).

Particular attention was dedicated to archaeological properties right from the beginning of the project, on account of their significance and incidence in the

[4] This first cataloguing survey was financed through funds made available by the law 84/1990 and in subsequent years by the Ministero per i Beni Culturali and by several Regional authorities with ordinary funds or European Community funds.

framework of Italian heritage but mainly because of their well-known characteristic features which require adequately adapted planning (Melucco Vaccaro 1987. Melucco Vaccaro 1992, pp. 18-21). Specific data forms for the assessment of the state of conservation of archaeological complexes and monuments were therefore prepared; the structure of these forms is in line with that of the forms conceived for historical properties but it also reflects all the necessary distinctions that characterize the more ancient heritage. The assessment of the state of conservation of an archaeological monument is therefore based on the semiotics of traditional damages – described using standardized terminology[5] – but also on the characteristics of materials used[6] and on the presence and efficiency of a number of "external" elements that are considered essential for the conservation of a monument: active and passive protection systems, temporary protection measures, rain-water flow and drainage systems, ordinary maintenance and weed killing, security systems and custody.

In order to formulate an information processing algorithm that would adequately calculate the vulnerability index of both ancient and historical monuments, it was decided, during the preliminary phases of the project, to focus only on built elements and exclude even in the initial theoretical speculations, particular typologies of archaeological properties such as the prehistoric and underwater ones. For this reason the survey of rock engravings in Valle Camonica is considered experimental in that it was an attempt to apply methodologies tested on ancient edifices to a very different type of assets. An heterogeneous sample of rocks was examined so as to document different geographical, administrative and environmental situations. Thus the conservation forms were used to study a number of rocks in the National Park of Luine,[7] in the Rock Engravings National Park of Naquane,[8] boulders 1 and 2 in Cemmo, rock 12c in Seradina, the rock of the map in Bedolina and other engraved rocks in Valtellina.[9] Mapping of the different situations was carried out using existing photographs and surveys; surfaces were sketched on the spot, in the case of rocks that had not yet been surveyed at that time.

The survey indicated that the engraved rocks suffered mainly from biological and physical-mechanical deterioration. In most cases, biodegradation and erosion phenomena were associated and synergic.

The greatest and most evident problem was certainly biological degradation, mainly caused by the presence of various indigenous plants, weeds, leafy and powdery lichens, ever present in cracks and on rock surfaces, moss and most particularly algae, mainly cyanophytic algae, which cause very noticeable chromatic alterations that often hinder the readability of the engravings. Biological damage is closely related to a number of factors: first of all, the *environmental situation* of the rocks – woodlands, in most cases untended, can deeply influence the intensity and type of biological attack and so does the formation of earthy and organic deposits. The rocks that were found to be in the best state of conservation, from a biological standpoint, were undoubtedly those in protected areas, where maintenance is carried out fairly regularly. Among these, better still were the rocks that had been subjected to adequate conservation treatment, which apart from improving their general condition also optimized their readability and, consequently, their accessibility.

Also *rock conformation* greatly influences the development of this type of deterioration: pronounced inclination of the lithoid surfaces, for instance, favours the formation of passageways for rain water flow, where a blackish algal patina collects, as can be seen on rock 12 in Seradina; the same phenomenon occurs where rain water stagnates on concave surfaces, as is the case for the map in Bedolina.

The situation in Luine, where biological damage was particularly evident, showed that the problem is closely related also to the *nature and lithoid characteristics of the engraved rocks*; in the Darfo-Boario area, for instance, emerged rocks are part of a different outcrop from those in the area of Capo di Ponte, certainly more friable and coarser grained.

Furthermore, in recent years (beginning around 1990) an increase in biological damage caused by greater *pollution* was observed.

Another problem brought to light during the conservation survey was crumbling and alteration of the rocks' superficial strata; these phenomena can be observed as erosion, scaling, exfoliation, cracking and even detachment, involving the possible loss of engraved details. Very often, detached parts are so historically accepted that it is impossible to establish – except in cases where indisputable traces of engravings are visible – whether they really had illustrated areas, or whether these portions of rock were discarded from the very beginning as being inappropriate for engravings.

Here again the crumbling and superficial alteration problems are caused by the presence/combination of a number of factors that are essential, intrinsic and external to the engravings themselves: the *rock's geological nature and conformation*, i.e. gradient, heterogeneity of the engraved surfaces, and orientation; *age of the engravings*, and duration of their *exposition to climatic agents*; the *combination of biodegrading agents*; *the natural environment*, in particular the closeness of forest trees and shrubs whose roots cause mechanical stress to

[5] Terminology used to define surface damages is taken from the CNR-ICR NORMAL 1/88, alterazioni *macroscopiche dei materiali lapidei*.

[6] Terminology referred to materials was published by Ferroni, Mariottini 1998, pp. 191-202.

[7] Rocks n. 6, 34, 101.

[8] Rocks n. 1-2, 50, 53, 57, 99.

[9] Roccia del castello nuovo, Rupe Magna a Dosso dei Castelli e Rupe degli Armigeri a Dosso Giroldo.

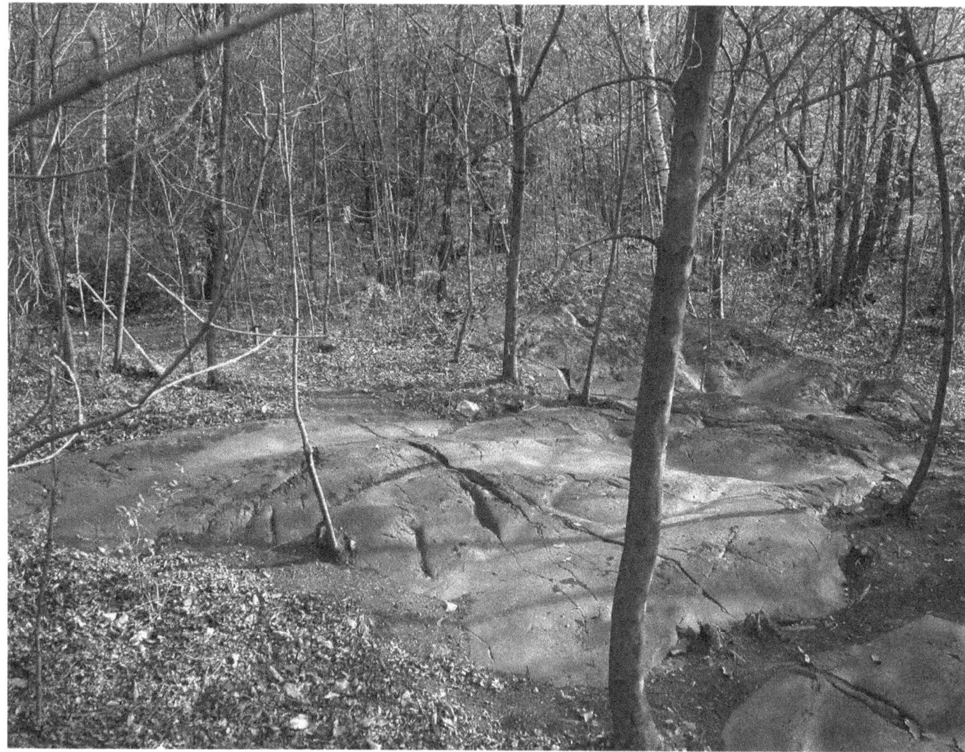

Fig. 1.4. Valcamonica, Parco Nazionale delle Incisioni Rupestri (Capo di Ponte, BS, Italy), Rock n. 24: the environmental situation can cause serious biological damage on rock engravings

the rock; *meteorological and climatic aspects*, i.e. temperature changes, rain, winds and frost which cause continued stress to the exposed surfaces; *pollution*, which, as we all know, accelerates rock surface deterioration. On top of these, also the *anthropic factors* must be considered; these are not only the dangers deriving from human presence, for example improper use, vandalism, unchecked trampling of tourists, which all favour and accelerate erosion, as we can see in Luine where, at the time of the survey, there were no signs or efficient protections for the rocks; indeed, among the danger factors, we must consider conservation or protective treatments carried out or not carried out, their adequacy, compatibility (see the use of inappropriate cleaning methods) and effectiveness. It was ascertained that the contrast method applied to highlight engravings by spreading casein and lampblack before the graphic recording of images (a survey method designed by the "Valcamonica Centre for Prehistoric Studies" - Centro Camuno di Studi Preistorici) favours the formation of micro-organisms. Hence the system, which the Superintendency had already forbidden in the mid 1980s, was definitively outlawed after analyses conducted on the materials and treated rocks.

The survey conducted in 1997 in the Valle Camonica was certainly neither exhaustive nor conclusive, mainly because it was an experimental survey; nonetheless, it allowed us to identify the major problems of the rocks' deterioration as well as the danger factors influencing the conservation of the engravings; it also set the methodological monitoring standards that were then followed in the computerized cataloguing project (IR Incisioni Rupestri – Rock Engravings), launched in 1997 and revised in 2001 by the Archaeological Superintendency of Lombardia and aimed at improving the management of this highly significant heritage. Preventive restoration and planned conservation must be based on a thorough understanding of the risk (Ferroni 2002a. Ferroni 2002b); the availability of this information qualifies the decision-making process and is of the utmost importance to set priorities, decide the allocation of funds and plan protection, conservation and maintenance activities, as wells as urban schemes in the territory.[10]

[10] After the cataloguing campaign in Valle Camonica, other experimental projects were implemented, aimed at testing the possible application of the system for the *Risk map* to other types of heritage. cfr. Ferroni 2003, pp. 8 sgg. Ferroni 2001, pp. 12 sgg. Also European Community funds were used for projects implemented in the framework of "Euromed Heritage" and the methodology used for the Risk map was exported to other European and non-European countries.: Accardo 2001, pp. 22-29. Accardo, Cacace 2001. All these data are currently being transferred to the web system with a view to improve their management and use on a national level.

As regards archaeological aspects, the form to record state of conservation was perfected and optimized over the years and a new, more specific, calculation method for the "vulnerability index" was also elaborated; a specific form to assess the efficiency of protective roofing in relation to the vulnerability of the archaeological assets was also elaborated.: Ferroni, Cacace 2004, pp. 466-472; MINISTERO PER I BENI CULTURALI, ISTITUTO CENTRALE PER IL RESTAURO, *Le coperture delle aree archeologiche. Museo aperto*, Roma 2006; in particolare: Accardo 2006, pp. 21-34. Cacace, Ferroni 2006, pp. 35-44. Cacace, D'agostino, Ferroni; Laurenti 2006, pp. 45-64.

References

AA.VV. 1976. Piano pilota per la conservazione programmata dei beni culturali in Umbria, G. Urbani (ed.), Roma.

ACCARDO, G. 2000. La schedatura conservativa: esperienze dell'ICR in relazione alla Carta del Rischio. In *Atti del 1° Seminario Nazionale sulla Catalogazione*, p. 34-45. Roma.

ACCARDO, G. 2001. Evoluzione del Sistema Informativo Territoriale nella dimensione regionale. In *Carta del Rischio del Patrimonio culturale*, Acts of the Italo-Spanish Seminar, p. 22-29. Roma.

ACCARDO, G. 2006. Coperture archeologiche e metodologia della Carta del Rischio. In MINISTERO PER I BENI CULTURALI, ISTITUTO CENTRALE PER IL RESTAURO, *Le coperture delle aree archeologiche. Museo aperto*, p. 21-34. Roma.

ACCARDO, G., CACACE C. 2001. Realizzazione dei Poli Regionali e gestione dei processi software. In *Carta del Rischio del Patrimonio culturale*, Acts of the Italo-Spanish Seminar, p. 30-33. Roma.

BALDI, P. 1992. La Carta del Riesgo del Patrimonio Cultural. In *La Carta de Riesgo. Una experiencia italiana para la valoración global de los factore de degradación del Patrimonio Monumental*, Contenido del Curso Internacional, Granada 16-18 diciembre 1991, p. 8-13. Jerez.

BALDI, P. 1997. Presentazione. In AA.VV., *La Carta del Rischio del Patrimonio Culturale*, p. 9 sgg. Roma.

BALDI, P., CORDARO, M., MELUCCO VACCARO, A. 1987. In *Memorabilia. Il futuro della Memoria. I. Tutela e valorizzazione oggi*, F. Perego (ed), vol. I, Roma-Bari.

BONIFICA, S.p.A. (ed.). 1996. *Carta del Rischio del Patrimonio Culturale. La cartografia tematica*, p. 11-62. Roma.

BRANDI, C. 1956. Cosa debba intendersi per restauro preventivo. *Bollettino dell'Istituto Centrale del Restauro* 27-28: 87-92.

CACACE, C., FERRONI, A.M. 2006. La vulnerabilità dei monumenti e dei complessi archeologici: schedatura conservativa e calcolo dell'indice. In MINISTERO PER I BENI CULTURALI, ISTITUTO CENTRALE PER IL RESTAURO, *Le coperture delle aree archeologiche. Museo aperto*, p. 35-44. Roma.

CACACE, C., D'AGOSTINO, S., FERRONI, A.M., LAURENTI, M.C. 2006. La vulnerabilità archeologica: efficienza e adeguatezza delle coperture di protezione. In MINISTERO PER I BENI CULTURALI, ISTITUTO CENTRALE PER IL RESTAURO, *Le coperture delle aree archeologiche. Museo aperto*, p. 45-64. Roma.

CNR-ICR NORMAL 1/88, *alterazioni macroscopiche dei materiali lapidei.*

FERRONI, A.M. 2001. Carta del Rischio e paesaggio culturale. In MINISTERO PER I BENI E LE ATTIVITÀ CULTURALI, MINISTERO ELLENICO DELLA CULTURA, et Al., *Il Sistema Carta del Rischio del Patrimonio culturale. Uno strumento per la cooperazione Stato-Regioni*, p. 12 sgg. Roma.

FERRONI, A.M. (eds.). 2002a. *The vulnerability of Archaeological Sites*, Rome.

FERRONI, A.M. 2002b. *Planned Maintenance in the Conservation and Management of the Archaeological Sites*, Roma.

FERRONI, A.M. 2003. Lo sfondo Carta del Rischio. In M. Ricci (ed.), *Rischiopaesaggio*, p. 8 sgg. Roma.

FERRONI, A.M., BIANCHI, A. 1997. I poli periferici e la vulnerabilità dei monumenti. In *La Carta del Rischio del Patrimonio Culturale*, p. 27 sgg. Roma.

FERRONI, A.M., CACACE, C. 2004. Carta del Rischio: la vulnerabilità archeologica. In *La Materia e i segni della storia*, Atti del Primo Convegno Internazionale di Studi, p. 466-472. Palermo.

FERRONI, A.M., MARIOTTINI, M. 1998. Lessico dei materiali lapidei. In *Diagnosi e progetto per la conservazione dei materiali dell'architettura*, p. 191-202. Roma.

MELUCCO VACCARO, A. 1987. Il problema archeologico. In *Memorabilia. Il Futuro della Memoria,* I. Roma.

MELUCCO VACCARO, A. 1992. La particularidad del problema arqueológico. In *La Carta de Riesgo. Una experiencia italiana para la valoración global de los factore de degradación del Patrimonio Monumental*, Contenido del Curso Internacional, Granada 16-18 diciembre '91, p. 18-21. Jerez.

MINISTERO PER I BENI CULTURALI, ISTITUTO CENTRALE PER IL RESTAURO. 2006. *Le coperture delle aree archeologiche. Museo aperto.* Roma.

URBANI, G. 1973. Introduzione. In G. Urbani (ed), *Problemi di conservazione*, p. 5 sgg. Bologna.

VALLE CAMONICA (ITALY) THE ROCK ART DATABASE BY THE MINISTRY OF CULTURAL HERITAGE AND ACTIVITIES-SOPRINTENDENZA FOR ARCHAEOLOGICAL HERITAGE OF LOMBARDIA: FROM IR PROJECT TO IRWEB

Raffaella POGGIANI KELLER
Soprintentenza per i Beni Archeologici della Lombardia, Via De Amicis, 11, 20123 Milano, ITALY
E-mail: raffaella.poggiani@beniculturali.it

Carlo LIBORIO, Maria Giuseppina RUGGIERO
Società Cooperativa Archeologica, Via Meloria, 22, 20148 Milano, ITALY
E-mail: carloliborio@tiscali.it, E-mail: mg.ruggiero@libero.it

***Abstract**: The rock art heritage of the Unesco site n. 94 "Rock Drawings of Valle Camonica" is safeguarded by the Italian Ministry for Heritage and Cultural Activities throught the Soprintendenza for Archaeological Heritage of Lombardia. In 1997 the Soprintendenza has started a computerized cataloguing project (IR, Incisioni Rupestri) which, as well as covering technical, scientific and administrative aspects, places particular emphasis on monitoring the state of preservation. On 2003 the application was improved, so that it can be used on Internet, with the possibility of de-localised data insertion (IRWeb, Incisioni Rupestri sul Web). Within the archive, careful and specific attention is dedicated to the systematic review of rock preservation state, which is considered fundamental for a medium and long-term heritage management strategy. The terminology adopted for conservation aspects derives from the Risk Map realized by Central Institute for Restoration (ICR) and Central Institute for Cataloguing and Documentation (ICCD) of the Ministry.*
***Keywords**: Rock art, Valle Camonica, IRWeb Project, preservation, management*

***Résumé**: Le Ministère Italien pour l'Héritage et les Activités Culturelles protège l'héritage des gravures rupestres du site nr. 94 de l'Unesco, "Les Gravures Rupestres de la Valle Camonica" par la Surintendance pour l'héritage archéologique de la Lombardie. En 1997 la Surintendance entama un projet de catalogage par ordinateur (IR, Incisioni Rupestri) qui couvre les aspects tecniques, scientifiques et administratives, et qui sourtout s'occupe de l'etat de conservation (de la roche). En 2003 l'application a été amélioré: c'est possible de l'utiliser sur Internet de facon à pouvoir inserer des données en n'etant pas sur place (IRWeb, Incisioni Rupestri sul Web). A l'intérieur de l'archive, l'attention principale est dédiée par un control systématique à l'état de conservation de la roche, puisque celui ci est considéré essentiel en vue d'une stratégie de sauvegarde de moyen à long terme. La terminologie adoptée pour définir les caractéristiques de préservation vient de le Mappe de Risque réalisé par l'Institut Central de la Restauration (ICR) et par l'Institut Central pour le Catalogage et la Documentation (ICCD) du Ministère.*
***Mots cles**: Gravures rupestres, Valle Camonica, IRWeb Project, sauvegarde, stratégie*

Valle Camonica, located in northeast Lombardy and one of Italy's most extensive valleys, is characterised by the world's richest heritage of rock engravings. In 1979, Valle Camonica and its rock engravings became the first Italian site to be included in the UNESCO World Heritage List (n. 94), for both the rarity of the phenomenon and the important scientific contribution made by the study of this rich heritage of engravings to our knowledge of man's prehistory.

The rock engravings, which constitute the site, are found throughout Valle Camonica (with a maximum length of 80 km and a surface area exceeding 1.300 km^2) on both sides of the Valley. More than 180 rock engraving localities have been identified in 24 of the Valley's 41 municipalities, with a total of at least 2.000 engraved rocks (at a conservative estimate). They are located at different altitudes: from 200 m to 1.300 m and also over 2.000 m.

The engravings were executed from the late Palaeolithic (9th–8th millennium BC) until the Iron Age (1th millennium BC), with sporadic persistence during the Roman and Medieval periods and later. The first comprehensive typological and chronological study of the valley's rock art, based on an analysis of the style, content and superimpositions of thousands of carvings, was made by Emmanuel Anati (Anati 1975), who classified the rock art into four main stylistic groups (Styles I-IV). This chronological system is still held to be valid, but over the last fifteen years has been subjected to partial revision on the basis of recent research and important new discoveries which have been made in the valley.

From 1955 to 2005, seven Parks have been created in this extremely rich cultural heritage, whose distribution in lower, middle and upper Valle Camonica varies greatly. These parks contain the main rock art sites: Parco Nazionale delle Incisioni Rupestri di Capo di Ponte; Parco Archeologico Nazionale dei Massi di Cemmo; Parco Comunale di Luine di Darfo-Boario Terme, contained within the Parco Locale di Interesse Sovracomunale del Lago Moro; Parco Archeologico Comunale di Seradina-

Bedolina, in Capo di Ponte; Parco Comunale di Sellero; Parco Pluritematico "Coren de le Fate" di Sonico; Riserva Regionale delle Incisioni Rupestri di Ceto, Cimbergo e Paspardo.

During 2005 was realized the Management Plan of the UNESCO Site, that requires collaboration between the authority responsible for tutelage and the local authorities concerned. In Valle Camonica, due to the immensity of the area and variety of the heritage, the preparation of the Plan regarded an elevated number of local authorities, all of which (given the limited time available) could not have participated directly. It was therefore decided to select as representatives the local district authorities (above council level), with which the Soprintendenza for Archaeological Heritage of Lombardia had already negotiated projects and programme agreements concerning this archaeological sector, together with the local councils whose territories contained the Parks listed above.

As for protection and conservation of the valley's cultural inheritance, these aspects are primary objectives of the Italian State, through the competent superintendencies, and of the local authorities. The rock art heritage, since it is part of the national archaeological patrimony, is safeguarded by a law (Legislative Decree in date 22nd January 2004, N° 42) which confers the responsibility for tutelage upon the Ministero per I Beni e le Attività Culturali-Ministry of Cultural Heritage and Activities (art. 4, c. 1).

The engraved rocks are mainly sited in wooded areas and they are at risk from factors related to climate and environment, both natural and in the form of human activity (increased pollution, soil destabilization which increases erosion) which can lead to serious deterioration of the engraved rock surfaces. This could result in the partial loss of this UNESCO World Heritage Site if suitable conservation treatment is not rapidly given.

In 1990, on the basis of the results of the first ten years' work, the variety of circumstances studied and the increase of deterioration measured (mainly due to the growth of atmospheric pollution), the urgent need to face the problem of deterioration through a systematic interdisciplinary study became clear. For these reasons there were two interlinked study projects to obtain a wide-ranging knowledge of Valle Camonica's many rock art sites (and those of neighbouring Valtellina, which also contains rock art).

The first project was the Study Commission on the Deterioration of Engraved Rocks[1] promoted in 1992 by the Soprintendenza for Archaeological Heritage of Lombardia. It performed surveys, sampling and analyses (lithological, biological, chemical, vegetational, climatic etc.) to define the geological, lithological and conservation situation of Valle Camonica's main rock engraving sites, investigating the causes and types of pollution, isolating the causes of deterioration (physical, mechanical and biological), marking out the plant species most widespread on the rocks, selecting the most appropriate products to remove them (already tested by the ICR for stone conservation), testing these on lithologically different rocks and monuments (Parco Nazionale delle Incisioni Rupestri in Capo di Ponte; Massi di Cemmo area; Bedolina area; Seradina area; Parco Comunale di Luine; steles and Calcolithic menhirs from various valley sites) and monitoring the results.

The second project was promoted in 1997 by the ICR and the ICCD of the Ministry of Cultural Heritage and Activities, as part of a national project to create a Risk Map of Italian Cultural Heritage (the results of this research are illustrated in A.M. Ferroni's contribution in this Workshp). This project aimed at an analysis of preservation states, and highlighted how the biological, physical and mechanical deterioration of the rocks was closely related to the human factors (wear by trampling, vandalism and rock cleaning performed by non-specialist personnel). The analysis revealed that rocks in protected areas, where ordinary maintenance is constantly performed, are clearly in better states of conservation. Hence the crucial importance of careful and regular maintenance, without which even the most rigorous restoration work runs the risk of losing its effectiveness.

The treatment of the rocks in order to preserve them, using methods sanctioned by the Istituto Centrale del Restauro, has been under way since 1980 only in the Parco Nazionale delle Incisioni Rupestri, Capo di Ponte. With the exception of a campaign by Darfo-Boario Terme council in the Parco Comunale di Luine on Rock no. 34 in 1999 and that by the Consorzio della Riserva on Rock 6 of the Riserva Regionale di Ceto, Cimbergo e Paspardo (2005), the State is the only body which has contributed funds for the site's protection and preservation with annual programs of conservation work.

In the last ten years the Soprintendenza has also started a computerized cataloguing system in order to record the rock engravings. This initiative concludes a lengthy period of study and experiment started in 1984 with the

[1] The Commission was composed by Soprintendenza for Archaeological Heritage of Lombardia; Soprintendenza per i Beni Culturali e Ambientali della Regione Autonoma Valle d'Aosta (a chemist expert in weathering phenomena); Soprintendenza per i Beni Storico-Artistici di Venezia (a biologist expert in micro-organisms); Istituto Centrale per il Restauro; "Gino Bozza" Centre for the study of the causes of decay of works of art and the development of conservation methods (CNR-Milan); Azienda Servizi Municipalizzati (ASM) of Brescia (a chemist and a geologist. Within this commission, the "Gino Bozza" Study Centre performed mineralogical examinations to determine lithological features and the extent of deterioration. The Municipal Service Firm of Brescia conducted a systematic survey of climatic conditions and analysed the air and polluting agents by means of a mobile survey station which was placed inside the Parco Nazionale delle Incisioni Rupestri in Capo di Ponte for six months.

IR Sheet[2] and continued in 1989 with the Petra cataloguing project.[3]

In 1997 it was created the Rock Art Conservation Monitoring Archive, based on a computerized cataloguing system called IR (Incisioni Rupestri-Rock Engravings), a tool for mapping and recording the patrimony and its conservation history with the use of modern techniques such as photogrammetry and digital photography. The IR System was later revised for use via Internet and Intranet and was renamed IRWeb since 2003. IRWeb constitutes a new development in rock art studies inasmuch as it was created as a modifiable and continually updatable inventory which is accessible and available for online consultation.

THE HISTORY OF THE PROJECT: FROM IR TO IRWEB

(Incisioni Rupestri sul Web-Rock engravings on the WEB)

The inventory system used for the engraved rocks was designed and created in 1997 by the Soprintendenza for Archaeological Heritage of Lombardia and has been applied not only to the rock art of Valle Camonica, but to all the rock art sites present in other Lombardy provinces (Sondrio, Bergamo, Brescia, Como, Lecco and Varese). It uses modern recording methods, such as photogrammetry, laser scanner and digital photography.[4]

In comparison with the rock art cataloguing methods used by other organizations which operate in Valle Camonica, the Soprintendenza's project is distinguished by the fact that the entire surface of each rock is taken into consideration, not just the area with carvings (or even each single carving).[5] This criterion is of paramount importance, because a detailed analysis of the whole rock permits a complete evaluation of its condition and thus allows the onset or aggravation of deterioration states that could cause serious damage – and thus prejudice its conservation for future generations – to be avoided.

This electronic archive, designed to allow monitoring of the preservation state and the programming of conservation campaigns according to the indications of the Ministry's Risk Map, contains an interactive database which is able to hold technical and scientific as well as administrative information together with photographs and drawings and may be repeatedly updated.

The database for monitoring the rocks' condition is created by means of the following steps:

1) data acquisition

2) research and collation of archive and bibliographical references

3) insertion of digital photographs

4) elaboration of computer graphics illustrating conservation data

5) database compilation

1) Data acquisition

The first step is to obtain the plan of the rock surface. The photogrammetry is fundamental because it yields high-precision drawings, with levels or in 3D (useful for the construction of scale models).

The data are then subjected to computer elaboration so as to obtain a vectorized perimeter plan, on which a grid of 50cm squares (referred to as "Zones") is superimposed: this enables individual engravings to be positioned with respect to the entire rock surface.

On 2005 the Soprintendenza for Archaeological Heritage of Lombardia applied the laser scanner technology on a rock placed in Bedolina (Capo di Ponte, Brescia, Italy).

At this juncture a series of photographs from different positions are taken in the field, so as to record the Zones and the Figurations and Scenes (i.e. groups of Figurations which together portray of events such as dances or duels, or complex entities e.g. cultivated fields and paths or villages) they contain.

[2] In 1984, on behalf of the ICCD-Istituto Centrale per il Catalogo e la Documentazione, the Soprintendenza for Archaeological Heritage of Lombardia produced two IR Sheets; one, for rock art (IR Sheet designed by R.De Marinis), the other, for steles (designed by R. Poggiani Keller).

[3] In 1989, as part of a detailed project for developing the Parco Nazionale delle Incisioni Rupestri and the Massi di Cemmo, financed by special Ministry funds under Law 449/1987, the decision to create a rock engraving data bank – which then did not exist – was taken, and the IR Sheets designed in 1984 were tried out on a sizeable sample. Taking the IR Sheets as a starting point, an archiving programme known as "Petra" was drawn up. This system organized the data in seven complementary archives: a rock archive, scene archive, figure archive, graphic archive, photographic archive, bibliographic archive and conservation archive. A study group was formed, coordinated by R. Poggiani Keller of the *Soprintendenza* and composed of specialists (Prof. Bertucci of the Università di Genova, Prof. R. De Marinis of the Università degli Studi di Milano, A. Fossati of the Cooperative "Le Orme dell'uomo", M. Simões de Abreu, L. Jaffe, M.G. Ruggiero, and C. Modi and C. Baruffi of Ikonos). A Terminological Dictionary was prepared, which served as the basis for subsequent lexicons. This archiving programme was interrupted in 1990, together with the practice of making contact drawings of the engravings (the principal recording method employed prior to the 1990s), in order to find methods that were more objective and rapid, so as to cope with the large number of engravings.

[4] The inspiration for the project came from A.M. Ardovino, at the time Soprintendente per i Beni Archeologici della Lombardia. F. Iozzi was responsible for software production and programming. The experimentation, development and construction of the database is due to C. Liborio and M.G. Ruggiero (SCA-Società Cooperativa Archeologica di Milano). Conservation matters were coordinated by L. Ghedin; photogrammetry was made by the firm FOART, Parma; assistance was provided by M. Pacchieni and C. Vaira of the Soprintendenza.

[5] Since 1994 F. Fedele noticed that in Valcamonica there are publications where the engravings are not linked to the profile of the stele or of the rock and that the morphological context is not studied (Fedele 1995, note n. 21, pp. 50-51).

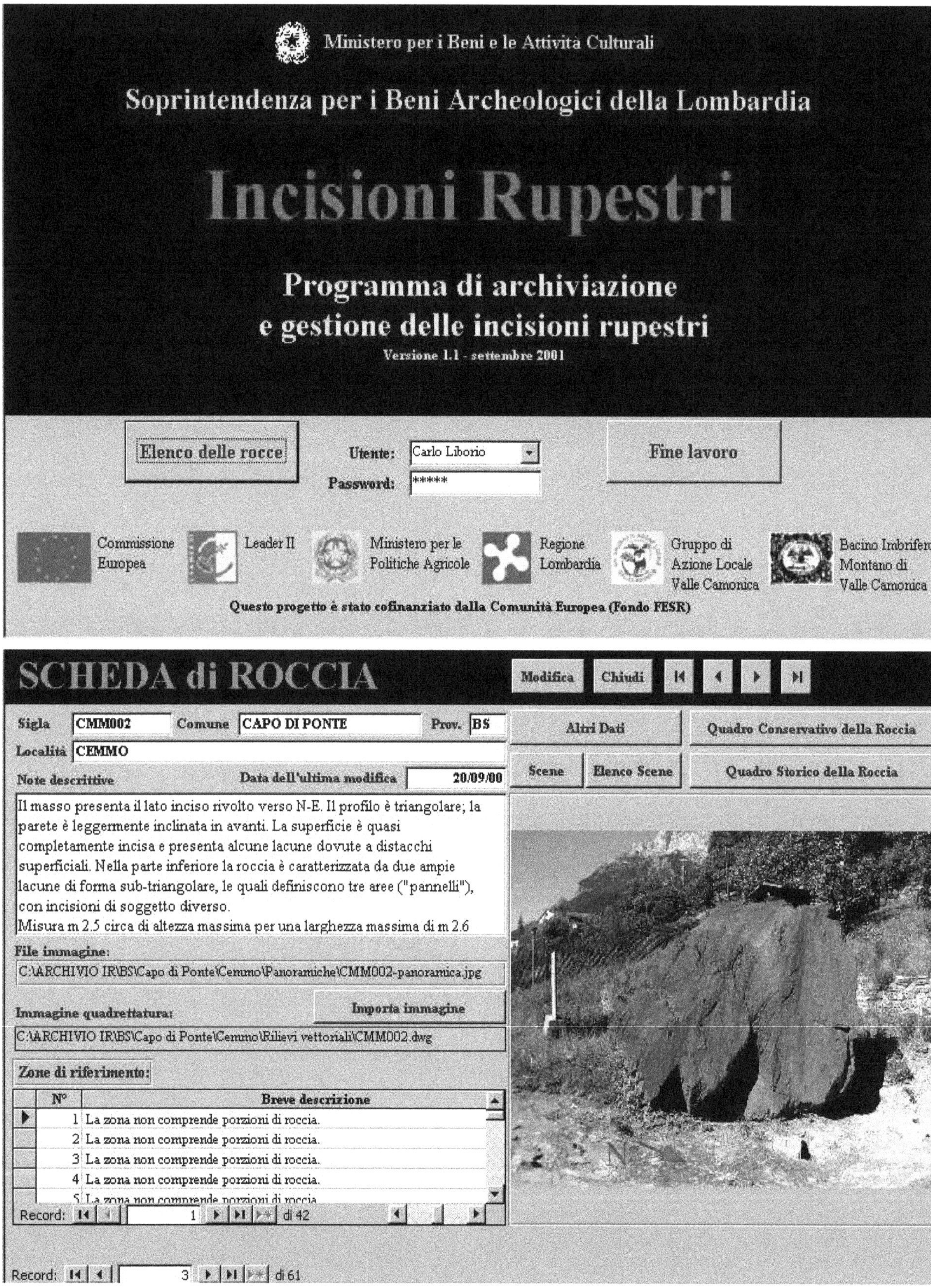

Fig. 2.1. The IR Project (1997-2002). The main page and the Rock Sheet of the data-base

At the same time, descriptive sheets recording information such as the morphology, dimensions, orientation and surface preservation state of the rocks, and the quantity, type and legibility of engravings present, are compiled.

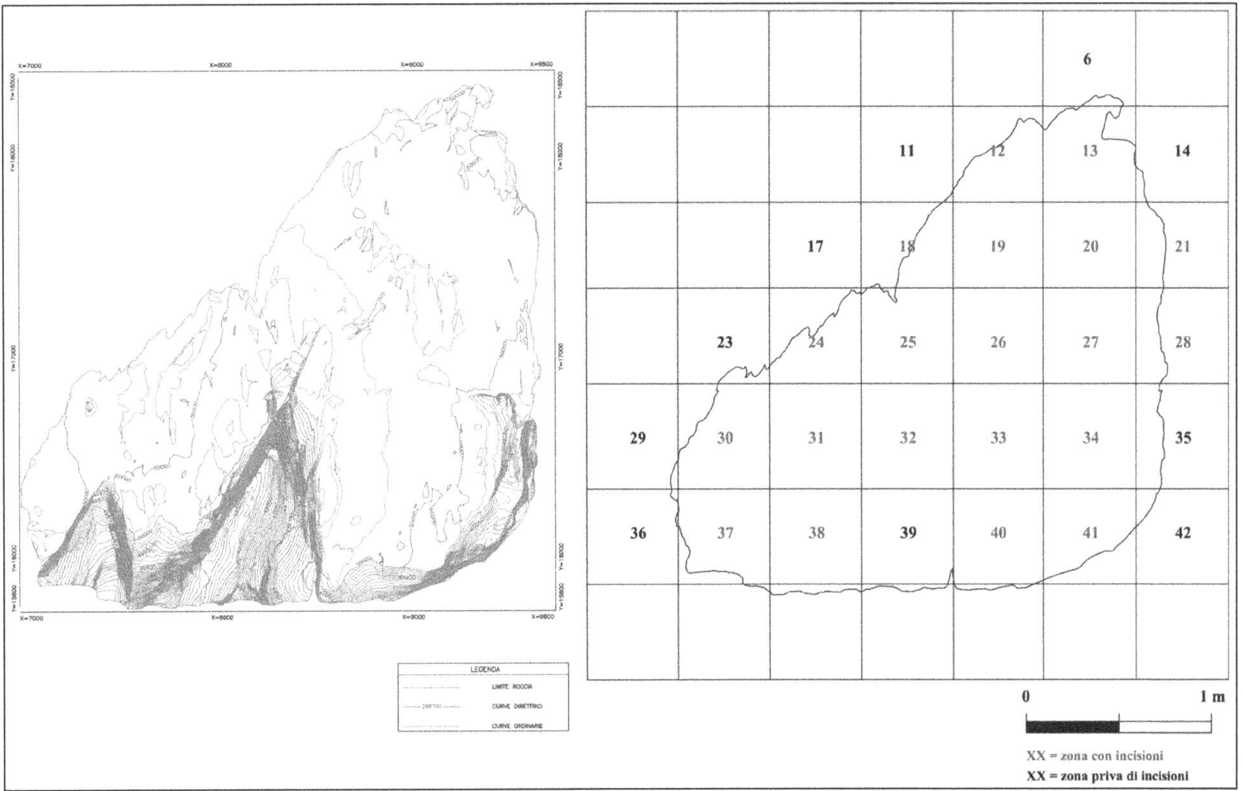

Fig. 2.2. The Cemmo 2 boulder: the photogrammetry relief and the superimposed grid with the "zones"

2) Research and collation of archive and bibliographical references

Contemporarily with the field recording, a bibliography search is conducted together with an examination of the Soprintendenza archives. The Superintendency headquarters house the Topographic archive, composed of written records pertinent to archaeological sites in Lombardy, and Conservation, Drawing and Photographic archives; there is also the Carta Archeologica della provincia di Brescia with the catalogue of all the archaeological finds. As far as Valle Camonica rock art is concerned, about 3700 drawings, 2700 black-and-white and slide photographs and more than 5000 digital photos are currently conserved.

3) Insertion of digital photographs

Every photograph taken in the field is memorized as a JPEG file (this is one of the formats approved for computerized inventories of archaeological finds by the ICCD). All the files are inserted in a central electronic archive, at present based in Milan, in the head office of the Soprintendenza for Archaeological Heritage of Lombardia.

This archive is structured in a systematic fashion: province, municipality, locality, photograph type (panoramic, or of a particular Zone, Scene or Figuration), rock code, brief photograph description. Each image file has a unique name which refers to the archive structure (for example: C:\ARCHIVIO IR\BS\Ceto\Foppe di Nadro\Raffigurazioni\FDN037-Z26 antropomorfo.jpg).

4) Elaboration of computer graphics illustrating conservation data

Information concerning preservation and conservation, in addition to being presented in detail in the Zone Conservation Profile and summarized in the Rock Conservation Profile, is available visually in files which contain the conservation state of each Rock Zone in vectorial form. The IR Project developed a method for the graphic recording and visualization of the affected areas and damage types, using the Autodesk programme AutoCAD: this methodology, was tested since 1997. The boundaries of areas affected by different kinds of damage are marked on digital photos, using symbols, and each damage type is memorized on a separate layer which is distinguished by a particular colour.

The use of digital photos allows, during the monitoring activities, to see and to verify the possible increse of the damages and so to decide the conservation treatment. These files together constitute a specific archive for monitoring conservation state of the rock art, located in the head office of the Soprintendenza.

5) Database compilation

The database is divided into seven descriptive sheets. In six sheets it is possible to insert photos.

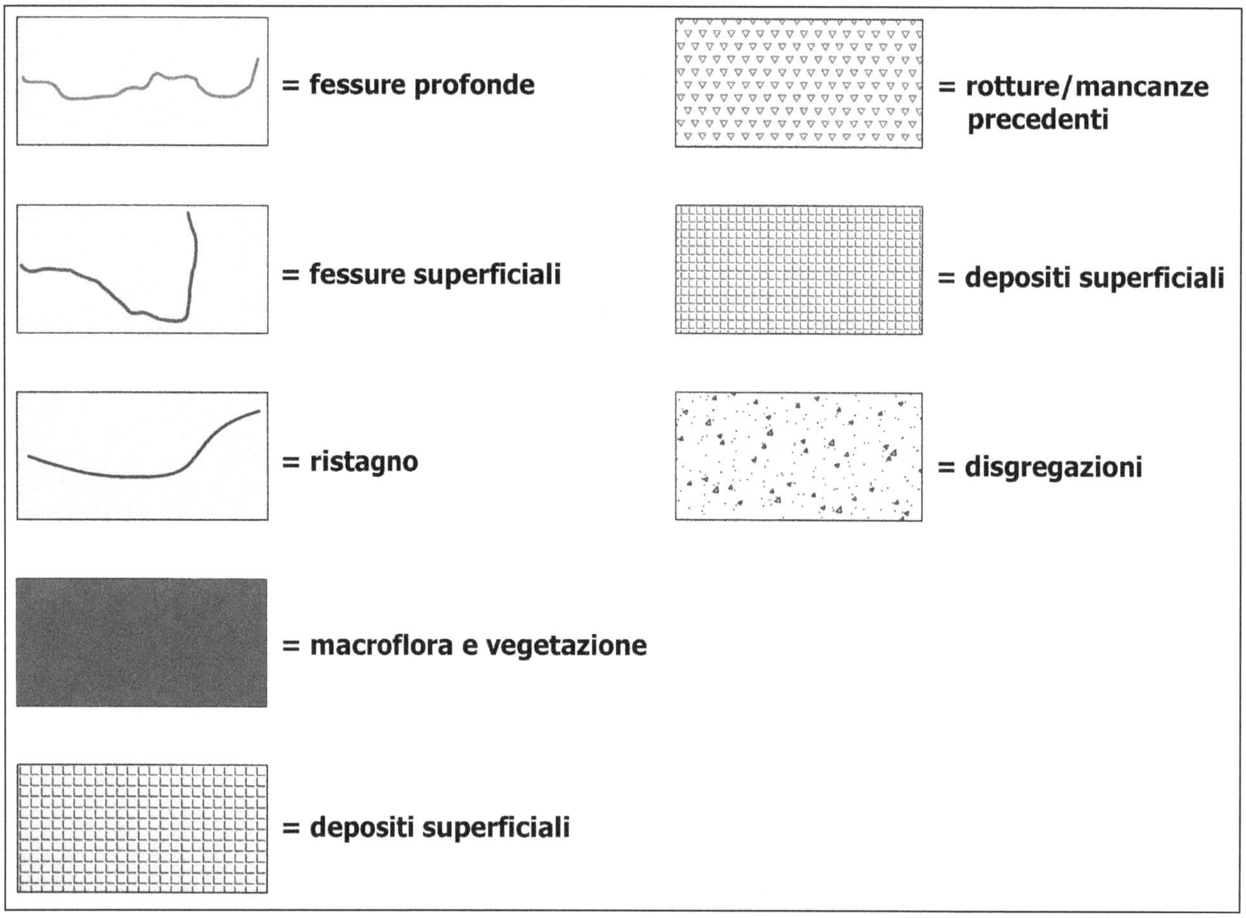

= fessure profonde

= rotture/mancanze precedenti

= fessure superficiali

= depositi superficiali

= ristagno

= disgregazioni

= macroflora e vegetazione

= depositi superficiali

Fig. 2.3. Some of the graphic symbols used for the elaboration of computer graphics illustrating conservation data

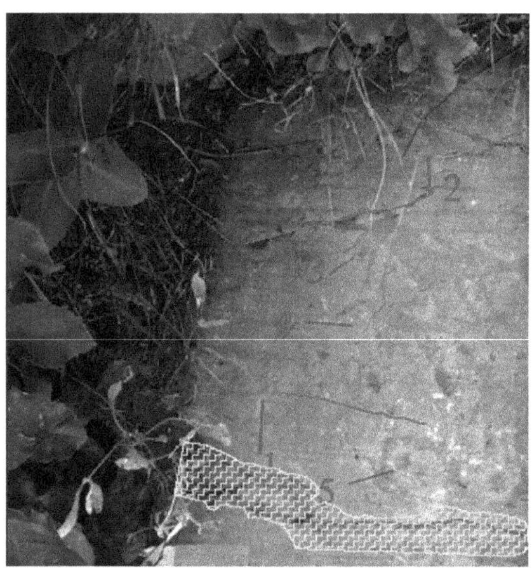

Fig. 2.4. Example of the vectorized damages

Rock Sheet: it is the nodal point of the archive, to which all the other modules refer. The morphological characteristics of the rock are described. The rock is identified by a code which makes reference to the locality and a progressive number series. A general photo and the vectorial drawing with grid squares indicated may be visualized. There are also relevant topographic and administrative information.

Zone Sheet: this sheet contains a brief description of the engravings present, with notes on the photographic conditions and indications concerning engraving overlays, when these occur.

Scene Sheet: it contains fields for identification codes, Scene type, engraving date and description. A digital image of the Scene may be seen.

Figuration Sheet: this sheet may be activated from the Scene Sheet and contains, in addition to the relevant identification codes, fields for chronology, technique, type and description. Here too, the sheet is completed by a photograph of the figure.

Rock History Profile: fields are supplied for a description of the rock, its discovery date, morphology and a summary of the engravings present and their chronology, as well as a series of archive data (bibliography, and photographic and drawn records to be found in the Soprintendenza archives).

Zone Conservation Profile: this may be accessed from the Zone Sheet, and contains a series of fields which refer to

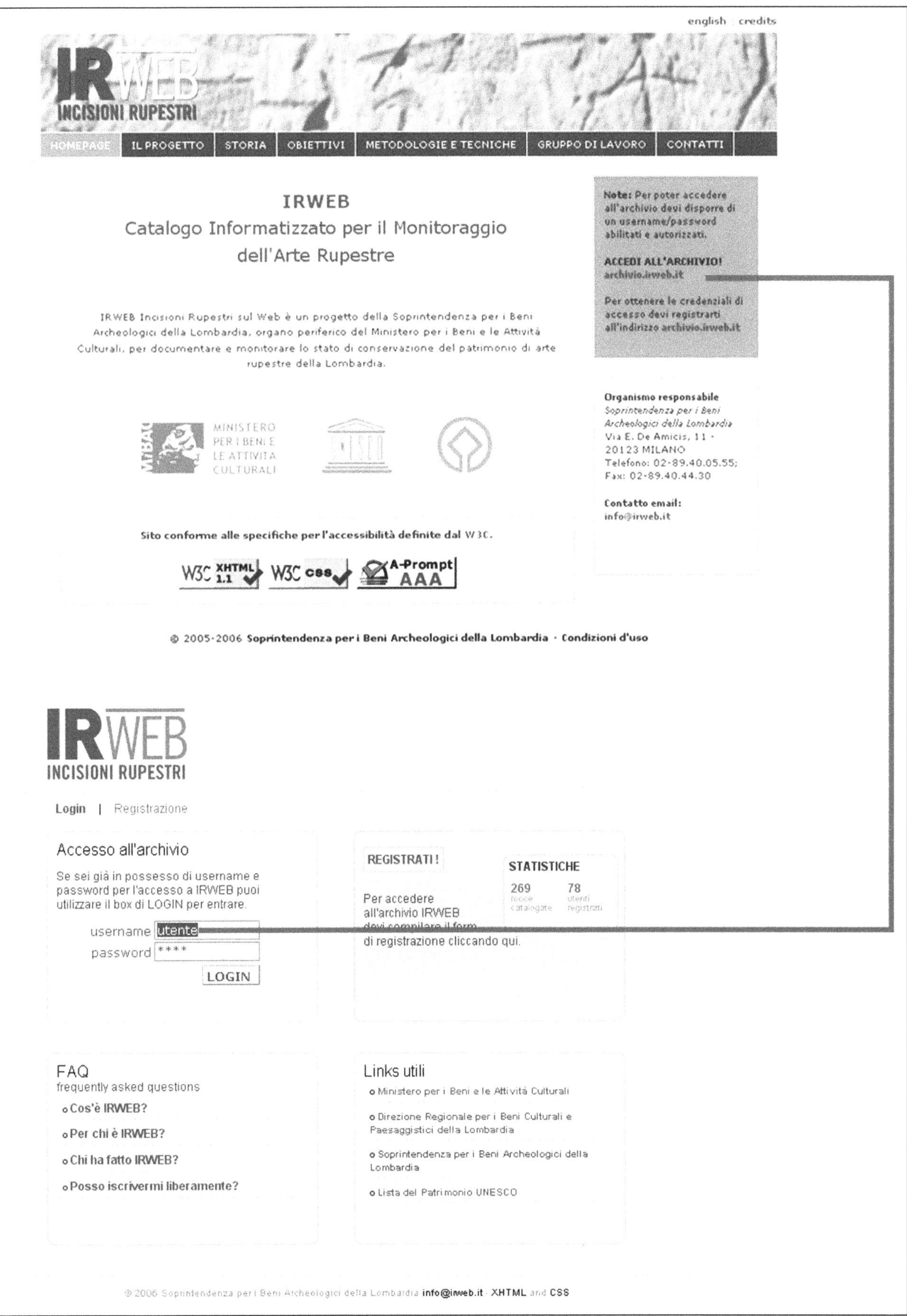

Fig. 2.5. The IRWeb Project (Rock Art on the Internet, since 2003).
Home page: www.irweb.it and home page: archivio.irweb.it

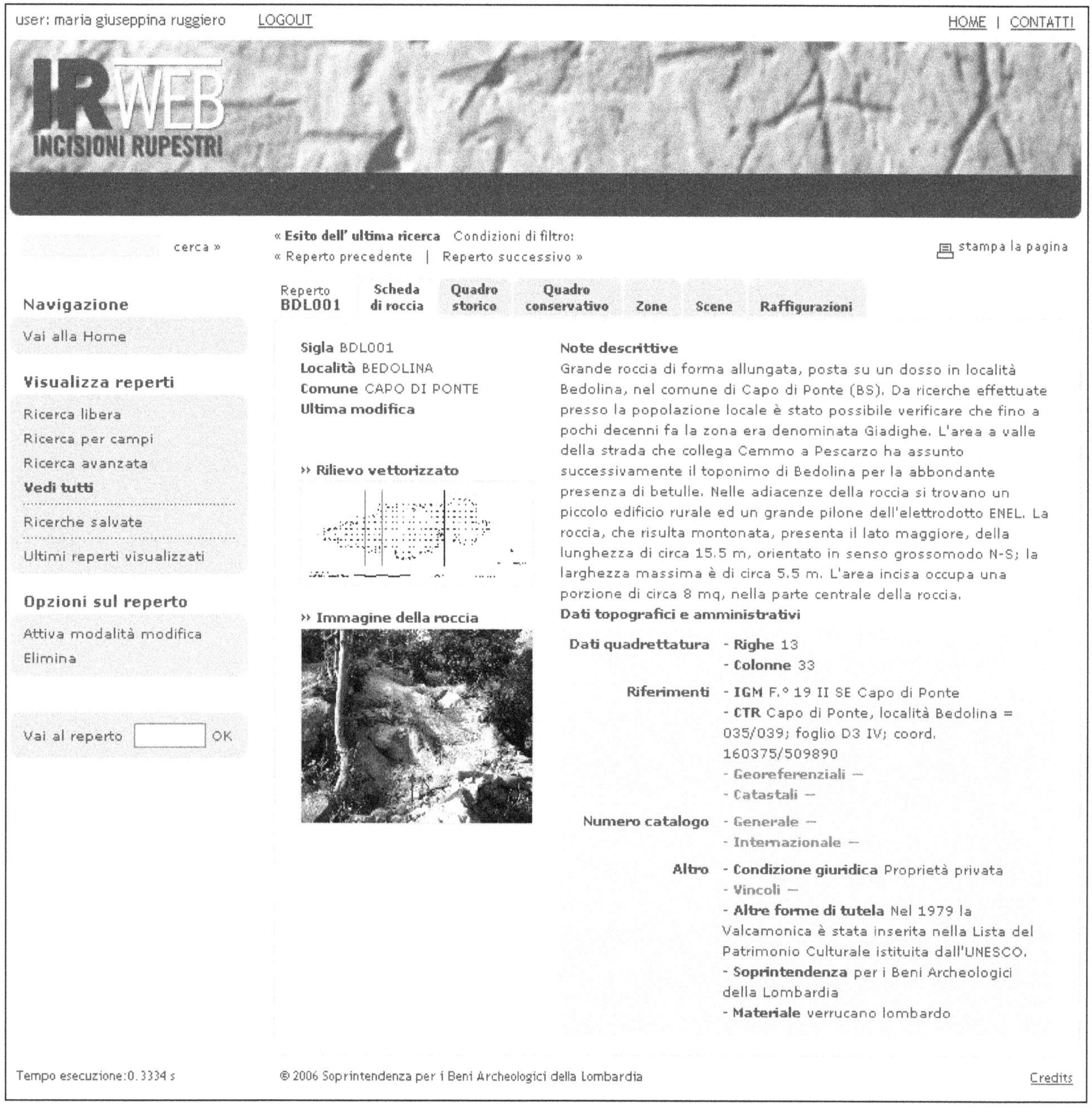

Fig. 2.6. archivio.irweb.it: Rock Sheet

the conservation state, the various different kinds of damage and the conservation procedures already carried out or under way on this particular portion of the rock. With reference to the Cultural Heritage's Risk Map, the terminology for damage to engraved rock surfaces ("intrinsic risk") has been used with some adaptation to the particularities of the patrimony in question.[6] The damage found in each Zone is summarized in the compilation of fields relating to the level of each damage type – and hence the degree of urgency of conservation treatment – in the Rock Conservation Profile. The collation of this information is thus of great importance for the short, mid and long-term scheduling of rock conservation programmes. It is possible to insert two photographs, showing the condition of the rock before and after conservation treatment; these facilitate periodic monitoring of the conservation state.

Rock Conservation Profile: the Rock Conservation Profile contains information regarding the utilization of the rock, the morphology of its geographical setting and notes regarding action taken with respect to conservation. Particular attention is dedicated to the rocks' environmental context, because the extent to which environmental factors may influence negatively their state of preservation has become clear. It contains information on the details of maintenance procedures, protection and safety structures, on how the rock is equipped for public

[6] A.M. Ardovino was responsible for conservation aspects and the adaptation of terminology.

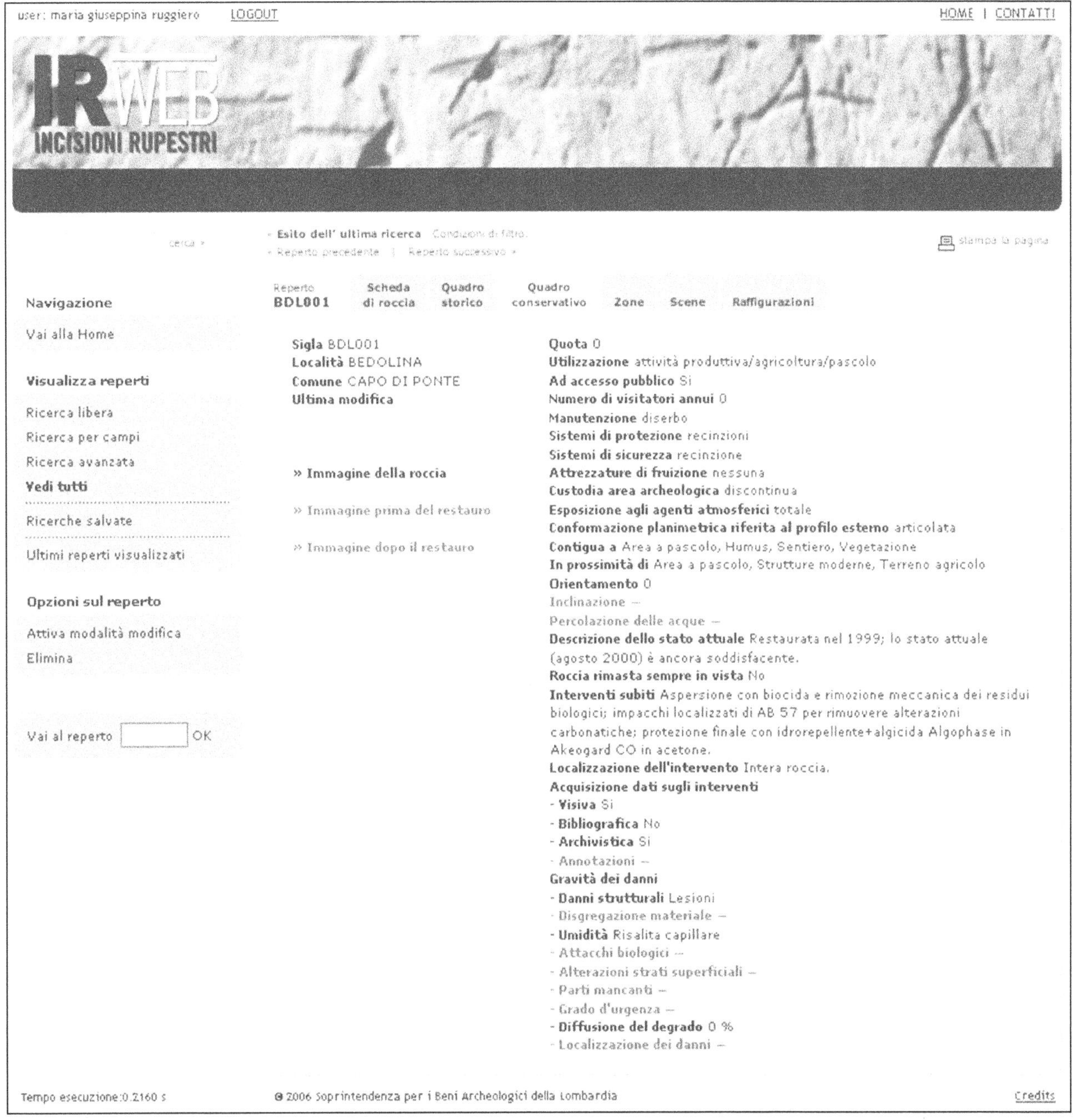

Fig. 2.7. archivio.irweb.it: Rock Conservation Profile

visits (walkways, explanatory panels etc.) and on the morphology of the surrounding terrain. The module is completed by data concerning the various conservation treatments, with reference to the gravity and extensiveness of the damage, and an evaluation of the degree of urgency of the procedures to be effected. The source of information regarding conservation treatment (visual, bibliographical or archival) is also recorded. The Rock Conservation Profile unites many data relating to factors of extrinsic risk.

The sheets regarding Zone and Rock conservation, because of their highly specific nature, can only be compiled by qualified restorers.

On 1997 the IR programme was developed using Microsoft Access but in January 2003 the Soprintendenza improved the database, in order to use it in Intranet networks and in Internet, with the possibility of delocalised data insertion.[7] From a structural point of view IRWeb is the natural development of IR, because it retains the same seven-sheet organization, with the same fields and the same lexicons for compilation; the data

[7] The system was activated on the Web by D. Vitali. Scientific consultancy, trials and data input were by C. Liborio and M.G. Ruggiero (SCA-Società Cooperativa Archeologica di Milano). Aspects concerning rock conservation and engraving restoration were coordinated by A. Sechi. Photogrammetry was made by the firm FOART of Parma and assistance to the project was provided by M. Pacchieni and C. Vaira of the Soprintendenza.

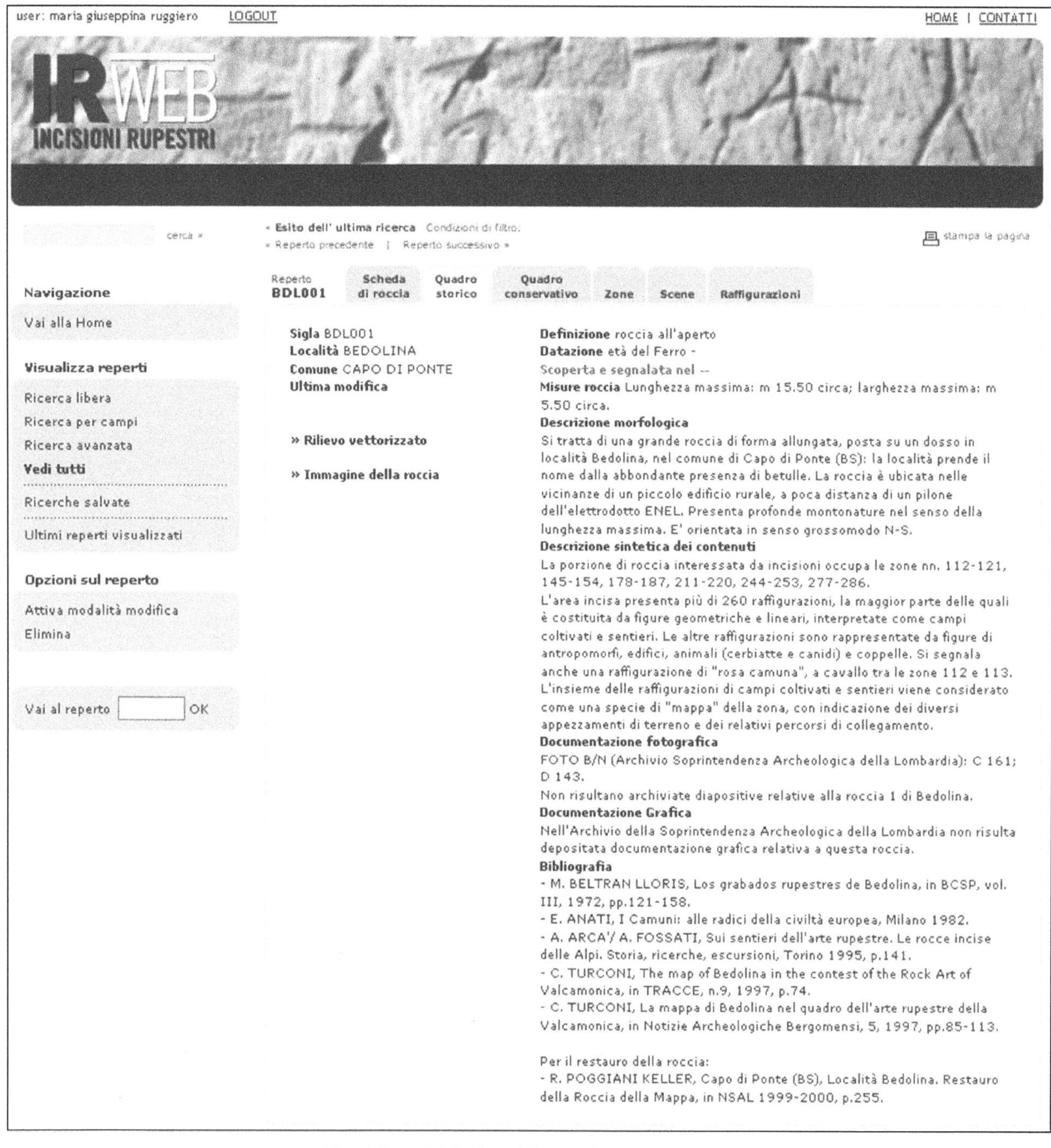

Fig. 2.8. archivio.irweb.it: Rock History Profile

acquisition procedure in the field is also identical. Naturally, thanks to the system's flexibility, it will be possible to implement the voices to be compiled according to requirements that emerge as work proceeds.

The new IRWeb programme was created using the most widely-used current standards, in order to permit the re-use of data in future versions:

- Database: SOAP interface with database, engine SQL compliant
- Interfaces: XHTML, XHTML strict for WAI (Web Accessibility Initiative) conforming versions
- Application language: PHP 5.0

It is based on a distributed client/server structure which is able to function efficiently in a high-velocity internal network (Intranet) or in a remote web server (Internet) and is remarkably simple to use, thanks to an intuitive graphic interface. The programme contains an online manual which facilitates data input and archive consultation.

Another advantage is that access to the archive is immediate; it is not necessary to install any software into the client computer, because all that is required is a normal web browser (such as Internet Explorer) which are by now pre-installed in most PCs.

With a view to data insertion via Internet, careful attention was given to the system's security, with the introduction of personalized access based on the distinction of various categories of user type, each with different privileges. The data visualization profile is chosen when a user or user group registers (login).

The administrator chooses between these interfaces: Compiler, Standard, Student, Other interfaces.

A fundamentally important feature of this new database is that all newly compiled sheets, including those inserted via Internet, are temporarily archived in a purpose-constructed Validation List. In this way the correctness of the data and insertion procedure can be verified and only after all data have been checked by the system "Superusers" are they integrated definitively into the IRWeb archive. This validation system has also the function of protecting the sheets of unpublished rocks or those under study, guaranteeing that the information is treated confidentially until the work is completed.

Particular attention was given to the safety of data, with the production of daily back-up copies and rapid procedures for data recovery.

After the phase of software design, the proper functioning of the programme was put to the test, by checking the inventory transferred from the previous version and by verifying the data insertion and consultation procedures.

In July 2003 the ICCD certified that the IRWeb system is compatible with its own cataloguing system, with regard to the close interplay between the descriptive data and the structuring of the information which the system guarantees.

In 2005, the IRWeb system was adapted to the graphic parameters for accessibility and usability indicated by MINERVA ("MInisterial NEtwoRk for Valorising Activities in digitisation") for public cultural websites. With respect to the accessibility of content, the system follows the indications of the Stanca Law (Law N° 4, 9th January 2004), which stipulates parameters that facilitate the access of those with disabilities to computer services.

In the web site -www.irweb.it- it is possible to know the history of the project, the aims, the methodology adopted and the staff.

In the web site -http://archivio.irweb.it- there is the whole archive for the monitoring of the rock art in Lombardia.

Lastly, it should be emphasized that IRWeb interfaces with the database by means of a WEB SERVICE, which consents the extraction from the database (after due authentication and authorization) of data in "unrefined" form, for use in other applications.

CONCLUSIONS

All data regarding aspects of conservation, visible in files which containing vectorized forms of information concerning the conservation state, are gathered together in an electronic Rock Art Monitoring Archive compiled by the Soprintendenza for Archaeological Heritage of Lombardia.

The methodology and first results of IRweb were presented in several congresses such as: 3° Convegno Archeologico Regionale, 22-24 ottobre 1999 Como; "Enter the Past. The E-way into the four Dimensions of Cultural Heritage, 8-12 Aprile 2003, Vienna"; "Quality for cultural Web sites. Online Cultural Heritage for Research, Education and Cultural Tourism Communities", Parma, 20-21 Novembre 2003.

Within the archive, careful and specific attention is dedicated to the systematic review of rock preservation states, which is considered fundamental and of vital importance for a medium and long-term heritage management strategy.

The collection of data with respect to "intrinsic and extrinsic risk" for the entire Valle Camonica and the other sites of Lombardia will enable an effective heritage management strategy to be put into action, and therefore protect the sites for future generations. Furthermore, the recurrence of particular phenomena of degradation or damage should permit the identification of standards which will guide the management and public utilization of this patrimony without allowing its condition to worsen.

In correspondence to the diverse circumstances, it would be possible, for example, to control the physical load capacity, regulating the maximum number of visitors or establishing an itinerary system which did not threaten to compromise the survival and exceptional value of this cultural inheritance.

References

ANATI, E. 1975. Evoluzione e stile nell'arte rupestre camuna, Capo di Ponte, Edizioni del Centro.

ARDOVINO, A.M., POGGIANI KELLER, R., LIBORIO, C., PACCHIENI, T., RUGGIERO, M.G., VITALI D. 2003. The rock art database by the Soprintendenza for Archaeological Heritage of Lombardia (Italia). In Congress "Enter the Past. The E-way into the four Dimensions of Cultural Heritage", 8-12 Aprile 2003, Vienna.

ARDOVINO, A.M., POGGIANI KELLER, R., LIBORIO, C., RUGGIERO, M.G., VITALI, D., TUMIATTI, T.

2003. IR Web: the online inventory of rock engravings. Poster for the congress "Quality for cultural Web sites. Online Cultural Heritage for Research, Education and Cultural Tourism Communities", Parma, 20-21 Novembre 2003, Auditorium Paganini. The text is on-line on the web site: www.minervaeurope.org.

FEDELE, F. 1995. Il contesto rituale delle stele calcolitiche camuno-valtellinesi: gli scavi di Ossimo (Valcamonica). *Notizie Archeologiche Bergomensi*, 2, 1994: 37-66.

POGGIANI KELLER, R., GRASSI, B., LIBORIO, C., RUGGIERO, M.G. 2001. Progetto della Soprintendenza Archeologica della Lombardia per un archivio informatizzato delle incisioni rupestri. In 3° Convegno Archeologico Regionale, 22-24 ottobre 1999, p. 453-463. Como.

POGGIANI KELLER, R., LIBORIO, C., PACCHIENI, T., RUGGIERO M.G. 2001. Progetto della Soprintendenza Archeologica della Lombardia per un archivio informatizzato delle incisioni rupestri. *Notiziario della Soprintendenza Archeologica della Lombardia 1998*: 33-34.

POGGIANI KELLER, R., LIBORIO, C., PACCHIENI T., RUGGIERO, M.G. 2002. Catalogazione informatizzata delle incisioni rupestri: il progetto Leader II. *Notiziario della Soprintendenza Archeologica della Lombardia 1999-2000*: 77-78.

POGGIANI KELLER, R., LIBORIO, C., PACCHIENI, T., RUGGIERO, M.G. 2004. CAPO DI PONTE (BS). Parco Nazionale delle Incisioni Rupestri di Naquane. Catalogazione informatizzata delle rocce, in *Notiziario della Soprintendenza Archeologica della Lombardia 2001-2002*: 31.

THE DIGITAL CATALOGUING OF ROCK ART ON WEB: SERVER-CLIENT ARCHITECTURE AND ON-LINE PARTNERSHIP

Daniele VITALI, Luca MEGALE
E-mail: daniele@oldsail.net, E-mail: luca_megale@yahoo.it

Abstract: *The paper describes the architecture of IRWeb's application, based on a distributed client/server structure, which is able to function in a high-velocity internal network (Intranet) or in a remote web server (Internet) context. The system propose a solution to common problems in cooperative online cataloguing systems such as multi-user security levels, data validation and publication procedures, grouped access to sets of data. All data is accessible via a standard webservice that enables IRWeb to be fully eligible for integration in external systems such as international public catalogues.*
Keywords: *Catalogues, archiving, photographic heritage, internet, web services*

Résumé: *L'article présent l'architecture de l'application IRWeb: celle ci est basée sur une structure repartie client/serveur, capable de fonctionner soit dans un réseau intérieur à grande vitesse (Intra net) soit dans le contexte d'un serveur web à distance (Internet. Le système propose une solution aux problèmes fréquentes dans les systèmes coopératifs de catalogage en ligne, c'est à dire les niveaux de sécurité pour les multiples utilisateurs, la validation des données et les procédures de publication, l'accès groupé aux ensemble des données. Toutes les données sont accessibles par un service web standard: IRWeb devient donc entièrement compatible en vue d'une intégration dans des systèmes externes tels que les catalogues publics internationaux.*
Mots cles: *Catalogues, archiver, héritage photographique, Internet, services web*

INTRODUCTION

Technical instruments available to non technicians approaching the building of a digital catalogue often aren't satisfying in term of scalability or security, and these are only two features of the tens that need to be considered. This paper is the outcome of a study done for the building of the catalogue engine called IRWEB[1] that has been made both from engineers[2] and archaeologist. We focus on the main features that need to be considered when developing, or choosing, among the existing solutions, a catalogue system.

SCENARIO

The planned system need to be fully "web compliant". It means that it has to run in a multiuser environment, and must rely on internet for the communications management. Old-style PC programs that run on a single computer are the most used catalogue system by now (2006). Who hasn't used a Microsoft Access® database[3] interface or a Filemaker®[4] programmed database? There is no problem with those applications (they are good for most uses, and perfect for experimental applications) but sometimes the choice is done taking a little too many compromises, often on scalability and security.

An internet based system can guarantee data availability. It means that it potentially can dispatch information to anybody that has a permanent or temporary (using asynchronous mechanisms) internet connection.

Placing a catalogue on the internet enlarges the security problem. Unexperienced people may thing that by placing valuable data on the internet it is a matter of time before it will become public. Current security systems can make it very hard to 'steal' valuable data, if managed in the right way. The whole deployment architecture needs to be planned with data security in mind.

Different discourses must be done for private or public databases: it's easy to understand why the second are widely more exposed to security threats than the first. The data security problem is a task for technicians, people deploying a data intensive application on the web should make sure that an expert evaluates the system, and not underestimate the task.

DATA AVAILABILITY (Fig. 3.1)

Until the spread of the internet all researchers had to cope with the problem of the access to remote paper archives. Being continuously connected each other enables a new world of communication. New catalogue systems must not aim to fully substitute paper archives, but to integrate and bring to full potential all contained valuble informations.

A web based system can assure full data availability. Anybody that has access anytime to an internet connection is a potential user of the catalogue system. The

---

[1] IRWEB 2.0 Informations, http://www.irweb.it, last accessed 2006-10-14; IRWEB 2.0 Public Archive, http://archivio.irweb.it, last accessed 2006-10-14.
[2] Simplecube Consulting, http://www.simplecube.net, last accessed 2006-10-14.
[3] *Microsoft® Office Access*, http://office.microsoft.com/access/, last accessed 2006-10-14.
[4] *Filemaker®*, http://www.filemaker.com/, last accessed 2006-10-14.

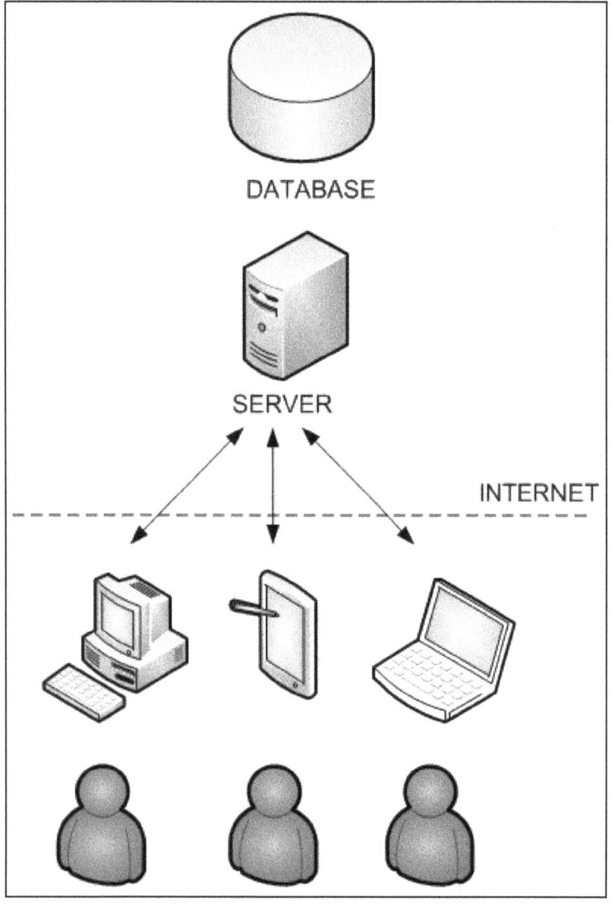

Fig. 3.1. Server/client architecture

application can be accessed anytime, anywhere. Data availability must not be intended only for people. External software systems may need to browse, request and obtain data from the system.

Availability for users

In a dynamic context such as the filling of a catalogue, in which many people from different cities, countries and expertise need to cooperate, the "thin client" model is the best suited. It is based on a standard server/client architecture, in which all application logic is done on the server and the client is only responsible of rendering the user interface. It means that all data and the effective 'program' stands remotely (on the server), and any client can be used upon authentication (your computer, using Internet Explorer). This architecture allows multiple user access to data.

Availability for Information Systems

Availability must not be guaranteed only for users. Third parties systems must be able to connect in a multi-standard environment, and flexible authentication rules must be enforced. The most widespread is the Web Services architecture, that requires communications (requests and responses) to be in the XML format. For example, the system must be able to export data in the OAI-PMH Web Service compliant format (a widely used standard for archives data exchange). It's important to plan an architecture that can comply with many different Web Services.[5]

It's not unusual to need to cooperate with different systems at the same time. There are many standards to comply with when planning a new system. The rule is: the more standards you enforce, the more interoperable your data will be. Standards are present at any level: from the single metadata to entire architectures.[6] For example, when describing a set of records in the OAI-PMH architecture there are many different standard techniques that can be used: the Dublin Core metadata descriptors,[7] the Encoded Archival Description[8] or WSDL[9] for Web Service general description.

Data availability can be achieved. A strong architecture can assure it for human targets, and standard compliance can do the same for third parties Web Services (Fig. 3.2).

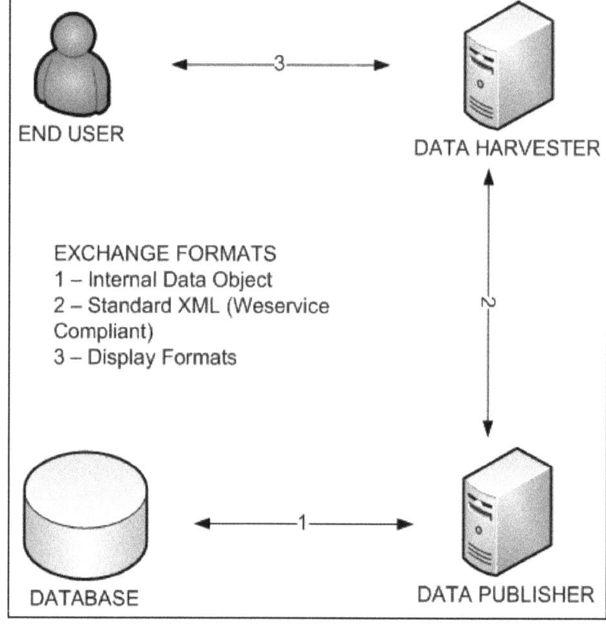

Fig. 3.2. Standard Web Service Architecture

IRWEB implements a Web Service Architecture, and uses a standard XML protocol to interact with the database (Fig. 3.3).

[5] OAI-PMH, http://www.openarchives.org/OAI/2.0/, last accessed 2006-10-14.

[6] W3C. *Web Content Accessibility Guidelines*. http://www.w3.org/TR/WAI-WEBCONTENT/, last access 2006-10-14.

[7] *Dublin Core Metadata Initiative*, http://dublincore.org/, last accessed 2006-10-14.

[8] *Encoded Archival Description*, http://www.loc.gov/ead/, last access 2006-10-14.

[9] Christensen E., Curbera F., Meredith G., Weerawarana S., *Web Service Description Language*, http://www.w3.org/TR/wsdl, last access 2006-10-14.

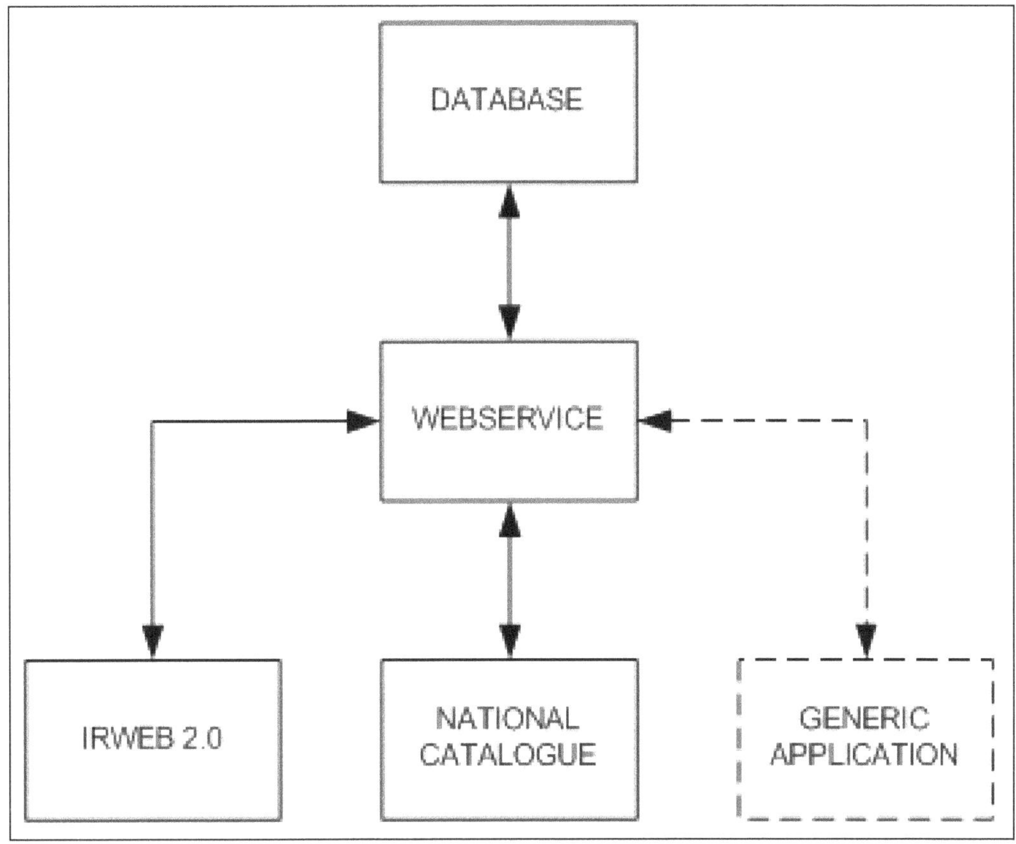

Fig. 3.3. IRWEB Web Service Architecture

GUARANTEE REUSE OF DATA

Archives contain valuable data. Its value is determined by quantity, quality, spent human and financial resources and reusability. Closed databases that can be accessed or modified only by creators strongly diminish their value. For example, a Filemaker® database makes very expensive to publish data on the web, since it does not implements data and interfaces exports to standard SQL compliant databases.

Again standards solve this problem. Once the matter was to find good relational database solution that was not expensive as the commercial industrial solutions (for example Oracle, DB2). Now almost all DBMS software implement a good relational engine, and the problem has lead to data storage quality. For small databases a full XML DBMS would be the definitive solution: stored data is directly accessible from source. For larger databases a DBMS with internal data management is needed for performance matters. Still, a full SQL Compliant database permits simple SQL exports, allowing fast and unexpensive reuse of data. IRWEB uses the MySQL 5.0 relational database.

There is also a methodological problem behind reuse of data. Using a top-class relational SQL compliant database is not enough. A strong data model must be created before actual realization of the database, software community offers many modeling languages in order to do that. For example the Entity Relationship Diagram.[10]

MULTITARGET INTERFACES

Until now we have given some useful guidelines for secure and strong archives implementation. However, the perception of the system quality goes through the final user interface. A nice looking, usable and effective interface is needed in order to reach the goal. There is still a problem to face: different users may perceive the interface quality depending on age, education or environmental variables. For example, a child may not find interesting the way data is displayed to a university student, or the data may need to be displayed in different contexts such as museums or web browsers.

IRWEB supports multiple interfaces at the same time. It means that the system can be used in an effective way in different contexts from different users. Figure 4 shows the data flow from the database to the end user: the visualization mechanism chooses the correct interface to display depending on user profile.

The same mechanism is used for language localization: a visually identical interface can be displayed in different

[10] *Entity Relationship Model*, http://en.wikipedia.org/wiki/Er_model.

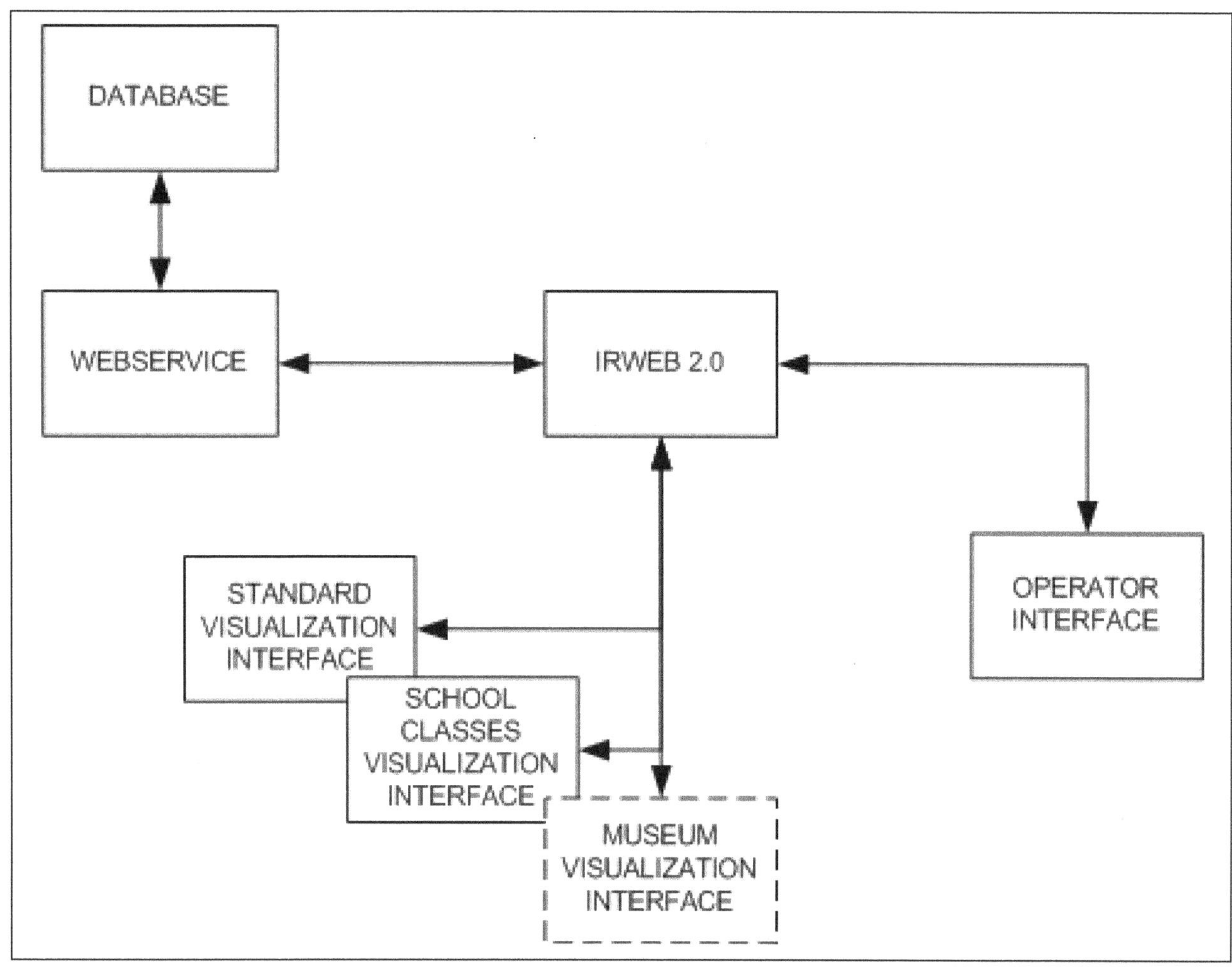

Fig. 3.4. Multiple user interface support

languages depending on user profile. For example, the view can be transformed from left-to-right reading mode to right-to-left, depending on the user habits.

A similar mechanism is used for accessibility: data is displayed removing all unneeded informations when accessed through a screen-reader, for example images.

CONTENT PROTECTION

Access control must be enforced in order to guarantee internal data safety and error recognition. However restrictive policies can compromise system usability. In bibliography we refer to Discretionary Access Control (DAC), Mandatory Access Control (MAC) and Role-Based Access Control (RBAC) policies.[11] DAC policies are based on user identity and rules (what the authenticated user can or cannot do), MAC policies are based on mandated regulations determined by central authority and RBAC policies are based on the roles that users have within the system and on rules stating what accesses are allowed to in given roles. Another distinction needs to be done between Open Systems (OS) and Closed Systems (CS). OS give access to data unless user is explicitly prevented from it, while CS prevent user access to data unless explicitly given.

The choice of the mechanism to use need to be carefully planned since it needs to be integrated in the system core. IRWEB is a Closed System that implements a RBAC access control method in order to be flexible and guarantee different access levels. Users are granted access upon registration and associated to one of the four roles: Guest, Operator, Supervisor or Administrator. Administrators can specify authorizations/rules governing access control. Data is grouped and users are grouped too. A second level of access control is enforced in the association of data groups to user groups. Figure 5 shows the incremental model for the first level role based distinction between users.

PHOTOGRAPHIC HERITAGE PROTECTION

Images often are the most valuable data contained in an archive. In web contexts images protection becomes a

[11] Samarati P., Vimercati S., *Access Control: Policies, Models and Mechanisms*. In *Foundation of Security Analysis and Design, 200.1.*

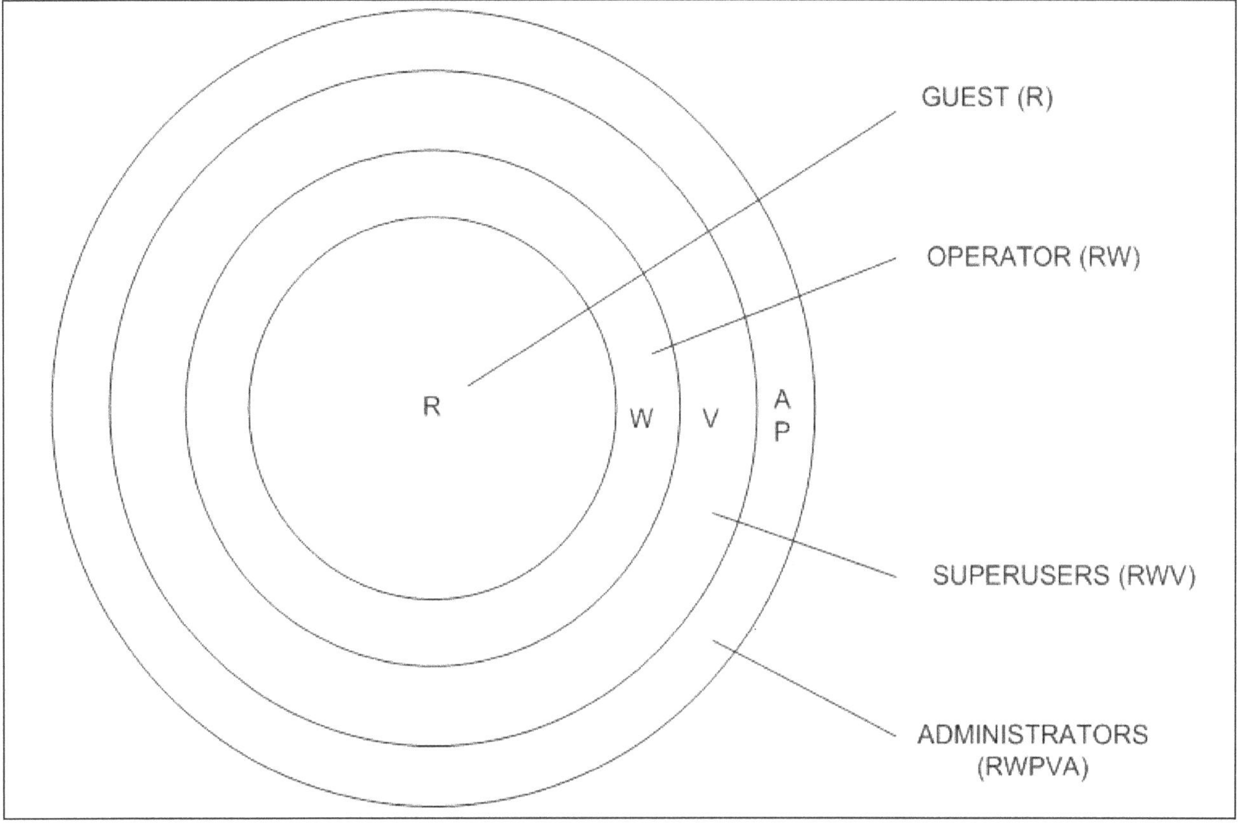

Fig. 3.5. First level role based user distinction

critical issue. If an image is seen it can be easily saved and reused. In this paper we introduce a good practice named *Minimum Needed Quality* (MNQ) that, combined with protection techniques, can minimize the abuse of digital images. Images are used for different purposes (i.e. didactic, personal, etc.) and the availability induced from a web context requires to protect the cultural heritage. Often high quality images are displayed to the end user for technical matters (i.e. the system supports visualize-tion of only one image format). The MNQ good-practice is based on a simple software architecture, shown in Fig. 6: the original high quality image is never displayed, and the end-user is shown a modified picture. The quality of the outcome is functional to: image usage, user roles and context variables. For example, an image needed for a poster need to be at very high quality, while an image that need to bee seen on a web page does need to be at the same high quality. Moreover, guest users may not have access to he first ones, while administrators do. The context also influences the output: images dispatched via third party web service may need to be in low quality.

Quality modification is not enough in order to guarantee full image protection: watermarking techniques need to be used and applied to the image before dispatching. Moreover, legal matters need to be solved such as license and ownership.[12]

[12] Vitali D., Megale L., *Digital rights management for archived pictures in web contexts*. UISPP 2006.

PRINTING

Archaeological archives need to cope with very different user habits: people are used to paper archives and sometimes is difficult to adapt to new formats. Printing is needed and it needs to be carefully planned. Paper formats of the contained data can be useful for the whole catalog building process. IRWEB supports multiple paper formats, in order to cope with different user needs. Two main types of formats are supported: *Work Prints* and *Full Prints*. Single item prints named "*work prints*" are made available to the operator with an easy-to-read report for on-site inspections, while Full Prints are a nice looking report of the actual contents to be used as an old-style paper format archive.

CULTURAL NETWORKING

Information sharing is the cornerstone of cultural networking. The European Community strongly promotes it and it can be considered as a good research practice. When planning new archives committers have the possi-bility to enlarge the community knowledge, for example by giving free access to portions of data. New techno-logies help this process by means of connecting people and giving free to use tools such as forums. Still, the value of a cultural network is determined by the quantity and the quality of information that is conveyed into it.

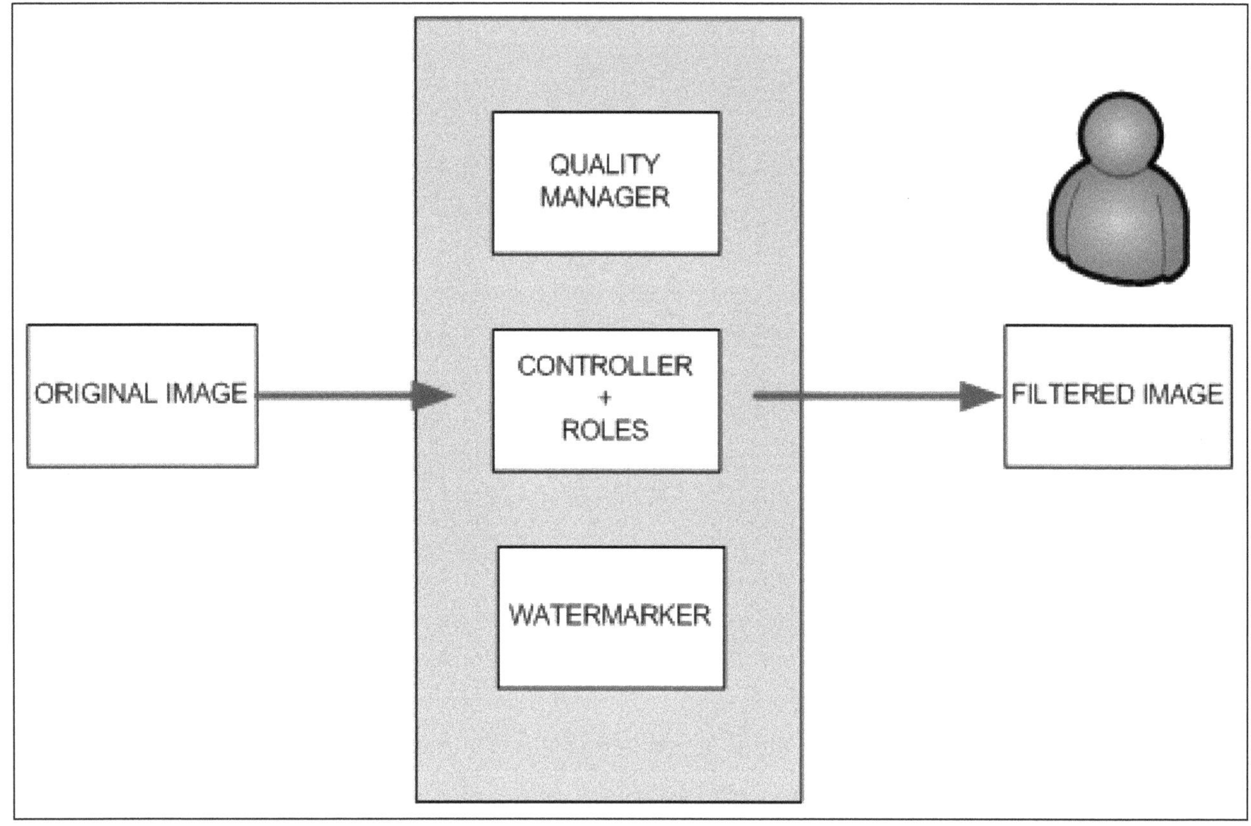

Fig. 3.6. MNQ software architecture

CONCLUSIONS

When building a catalogue system we all should keep in mind that archives should "*Make it easy for people to find, understand and experience their cultural heritage through digital libraries*" and "*keep today's digital content alive in the future*",[13] as stated in the main objectives of the "Information Society Technologies" section of the European Community Research and Development Service.

[13] Information Society Technologies, http://cordis.europa.eu/ist/digicult/index.html.

THE EUROPREART PROJECT – *PAST SIGNS AND PRESENT MEMORIES* EUROPEAN PREHISTORIC ART: INVENTORY, CONTEXTUALISATION, PRESERVATION AND ACCESSIBILITY

Dario SEGLIE

IFRAO/UNESCO Liaison Officer, Polytechnic of Torino, Dept. of Museography, CeSMAP – Centro Studi e Museo d'Arte Preistorica, Viale Giolitti 1, 10064 Pinerolo (Torino), ITALY

E-mail: cesmap@cesmap.it

On behalf of the Partners:

IPT – Instituto Politécnico de Tomar, Portugal; Asociación Cultural Colectivo Barbaón, Spain; CUEBC, European University Centre for Cultural Heritage, Italy; CSIC, Consejo Superior de Investigaciones Cientificas, Spain; CAOU, Cooperativa Archeologica le Orme dell'Uomo, Italy; UG, Gotland University College, Sverige; The European Centre for Prehistoric Research in the Alto Ribatejo, Portugal; UL, Université de Liège, Belgium; UDC, University College Dublin, Ireland: AJ, ArqueoJovem, Portugal; CeSMAP, Study Centre and Prehistoric Art Museum of Pinerolo, Italy

EuroPreArt Scientific Committee:

Luiz Oosterbeek, Andrea Arcà, Mila Abreu Simoes, Claude Albore Livadie, Maria Cruz Berrocal, Göran Burenhult, Hipólito Collado Giraldo, Ludwig Jaffe, Muiris O'Sullivan, Marcel Otte, Massimo Raffo, Laurence Remacle, Roberto Seglie, Alexandra Velho, Gonçalo Velho, Juan Vicent Garcia, Dario Seglie

Abstract*: This UE Project is focused on inventory, contextualisation, preservation and accessibility. The main aim of the project was to promote close international co-operation between the project partners and all other institution in Europe and around the world, devoted to Prehistoric Art. The broad range of Rock Art issued has necessitated the involvement of many important international organizations (IFRAO, UNESCO, UISPP). There is a growing understanding that we need to approach Rock Art management planning in as broadly based a way as possible: that is the way of principles of sustainable development in the field of Cultural Heritage preservation. We are now at the stage were we should re-assess each of our action, from the field work to the responsibility to disseminate knowledge through teaching and general educational programmes.*
Keywords*: Rock art, UE Project, inventory, preservation, accessibility*

Résumé*: Les buts principaux son liés à la considération que le Patrimoine Culturelle en Europe est lié à l'identité locale et des différentes régions et que le risques de destructions sont fondés sur l' aménagement du territoire, sur les transformations et l'impacte des éléments naturels sur l'environnement. La possibilité de considérer le passé comme élément pour comprendre le présent et pour projeter le futur n'est pas seulement un paradigme de la philosophie positiviste, mai est aussi la clé pour découvrir et conserver nos propres racines. En Europe, il y a de différentes situations de conservation du Patrimoine et de différentes réponses aux risques de catastrophes naturelles, comme les inondations, le feu, le tremblement de terre, la pollution des aires et des eaux. Le projet ArtRisk a voulu donner un ensemble de réponse aptes à faire front aux émergences qui peuvent menacer le patrimoine du passe et effacer la mémoire collective. Les partenaires, en complémentarité, ont développé et réalisé de différentes types d'actions, d'études, en produisant des instruments concrets.*
Mots cles*: Gravures Rupestres, Project de l'UE, inventaire, sauvegarde, accessibilité*

THE EUROPEAN PROJECT

EuroPreArt aims to establish a lasting data-base of European prehistoric art documentation, to launch the base of an European institutional network devoted to this domain, and to contribute to the awareness of the diversity and richness of European Prehistoric Art, as one of the oldest artistic expression of Humankind. It will improve methodologies on techniques of inventory, storing data, interdisciplinarity, networking and accessibility/diffusion, namely using new information technologies. The project will focus on selected clusters, from rock art to mobile art, from Palaeolithic to the Iron Age, from old stored records to modern field work studies. The project intends to create a model, introduce textual and image data, publish a guide of good conduct and present the results to the wider public on this web-site, open to other contributions of attraction of sites like Grotte Chauvet, or Valcamonica. The public's awareness is, thus, a mixture of false ideas (on "major" sites) and lack of understanding of the richness and complexity of this Heritage. It was based on these considerations that, over a year ago, a group of research centres and universities (IPT – Instituto Politécnico de Tomar, Portugal; Asociacion Cultural Colectivo Barbaon, Spain; CUEBC, European University Centre for Cultural Heritage, Italy; CSIC, Consejo Superior de Investigaciones Cientificas, Spain; CAOU, Cooperativa Archeologica le Orme dell'Uomo, Italy; UG, Gotland University College, Sverige; The European Centre for Prehistoric Research n the Alto Ribatejo, Portugal; UL, Université de Liège, Belgium; UDC, University College Dublin, Ireland: AJ, Arqueo-Jovem, Portugal; CeSMAP, Study Centre and Prehistoric Art Museum of Pinerolo, Italy) decided to launch the

EuroPreArt project. The project aimed to establish a lasting data-base of European prehistoric art documentation, including images, to launch the base of an European institutional network of units devoted to this domain, and to contribute to the awareness, among European population, of the diversity and richness of European Prehistoric Art, as one of the oldest artistic expression of Humankind.

Ultimately, it should contribute to improve methodologies on techniques of inventory, storing data, interdisciplinarity, networking and accessibility/diffusion, namely using new information technologies.

Community, and in many cases the authorities, have reached a good degree of consensus, that did not yet found its translation into a common code. The readers will not find such a code in this publication, but we hope they may find some useful and systematic suggestions.

In the duration of its first year of activity, EuroPreArt created and tested a data-base, made it accessible though the web and published a CD-Rom and a book. Its methodology and first results were presented in several forae, namely in the XIVth Congress of the UISPP in Liège, September 2001, and again in Lisbon, September 2006. Many other research units through Europe expressed their interest in using this tool and, thus, joining the project. A first improvement on the data-base is being finished, considering the obtained results, in the context of a research degree dissertation.

We conceive this effort in the context of several other initiatives led by several scholars in Europe, and namely in the context of the debate to create a closer network of European Prehistoric Art researchers and managers.

THE EUROPREART DATABASE SYSTEM

The EuroPreArt project has two mains goals: prehistoric art documentation and its diffusion. Its EuroPreArt Database System is the key to both aims. Development can be summarised in four steps: preparation, data collection, intermediate treatment and sharing data online. In all steps, specific archaeological and rock-art expertise merged with that of information technology (mainly data management, html scripting and Web design).

Preparation

The first step of the EuroPreArt project partners was to outline a database system, in the process, reviewing concepts disclosed in documents and meetings for more than two decades. Important sources include the files of CIARAO (International Commission of Western Alps Rock Art 1990) and WARA (World Archive of Rock Art), and a system called RAD (Rupestrian Archaeology Database). In this first phase, the project structured a "rocks file" with forms to catalogue each engraved or painted prehistoric rock surface, decorated menhir or portable art object. Future work will add a "sites file" and a "figures file", in order to achieve an integrated documentation path under a general sites-surfaces-figures structure. The main themes of this first file are related to environment, description and chronology of the "art", and analysis of the state of conservation, adding also as much information as possible about bibliography and intervention.

Data collection

Establishing a EuroPreArt data entry form was the second step. It runs under Microsoft Access (chosen for its availability) and has five tables (main, bibliography, keywords, links, institutions), seven tabs, 72 fields (numeric, text, logical and memo). The first two tabs data relate to location, geography (position, orientation, land usage) and proximity to any important natural or human landscape element. The third tab, probably the core tab, displays information about detailed chronology and detailed description of the "art" (style, overlappings, comparisons, correlation, technique, figures). The next tab is entirely for the bibliography. There is a pragmatic limit of 8 specific titles for each record but it is possible to insert as many titles as needed in the general bibliography. Bibliographical data are managed by the online site to generate three different lists: specific (surface or object related), general (country related) and total (the entire EuroPreArt bibliography). The fifth tab is for conservation: status (public, private), detailed description of the state of conservation and of the risks of damage, information about restoration, recording, site management and education. The sixth tab is for images: photos and tracings are not stored in the Microsoft Access file, only entries referring to separate picture-files kept outside the database. The last tab is for additional notes and information about the institution and compiler of the record.

Intermediate treatment

Beside this common structure, EuroPreArt partners worked on their separate geographic sets of records. Therefore, the third step consisted in manipulating various Microsoft Access tables, which were exported and merged into two main databases: "prehistoric art" and "bibliography".

Online data-sharing

The best choice to achieve the second main goal of the EuroPreArt project, its diffusion is the world-wide-web. The technical solution for this final step is a dynamic Web site, where a template-based structure dynamically generates pages in response to data retrieval requests. The final form, which obviously contains the same data of the original data entry forms, shows texts and pictures with a properly formatted graphic interface, readable and printable with almost any web browser. BASERUNNER

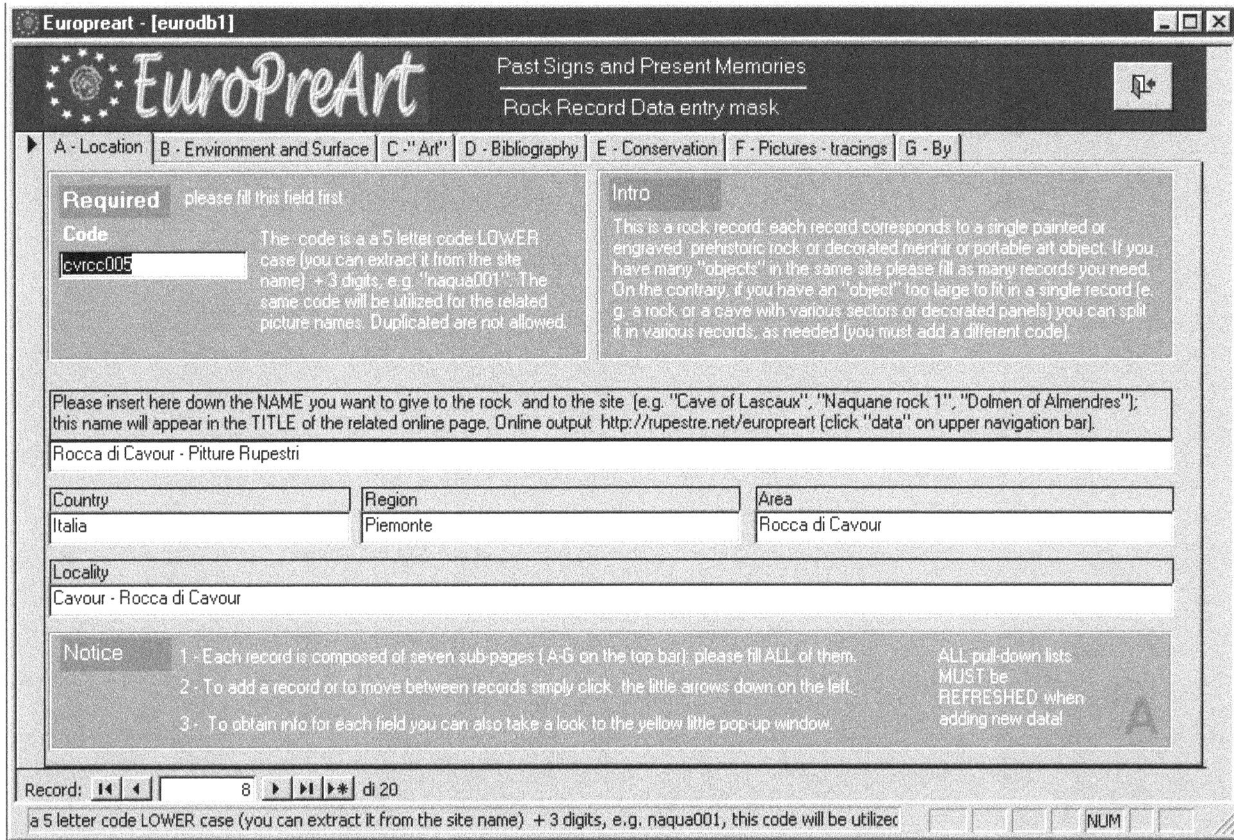

Fig. 4.1. Page A – Location

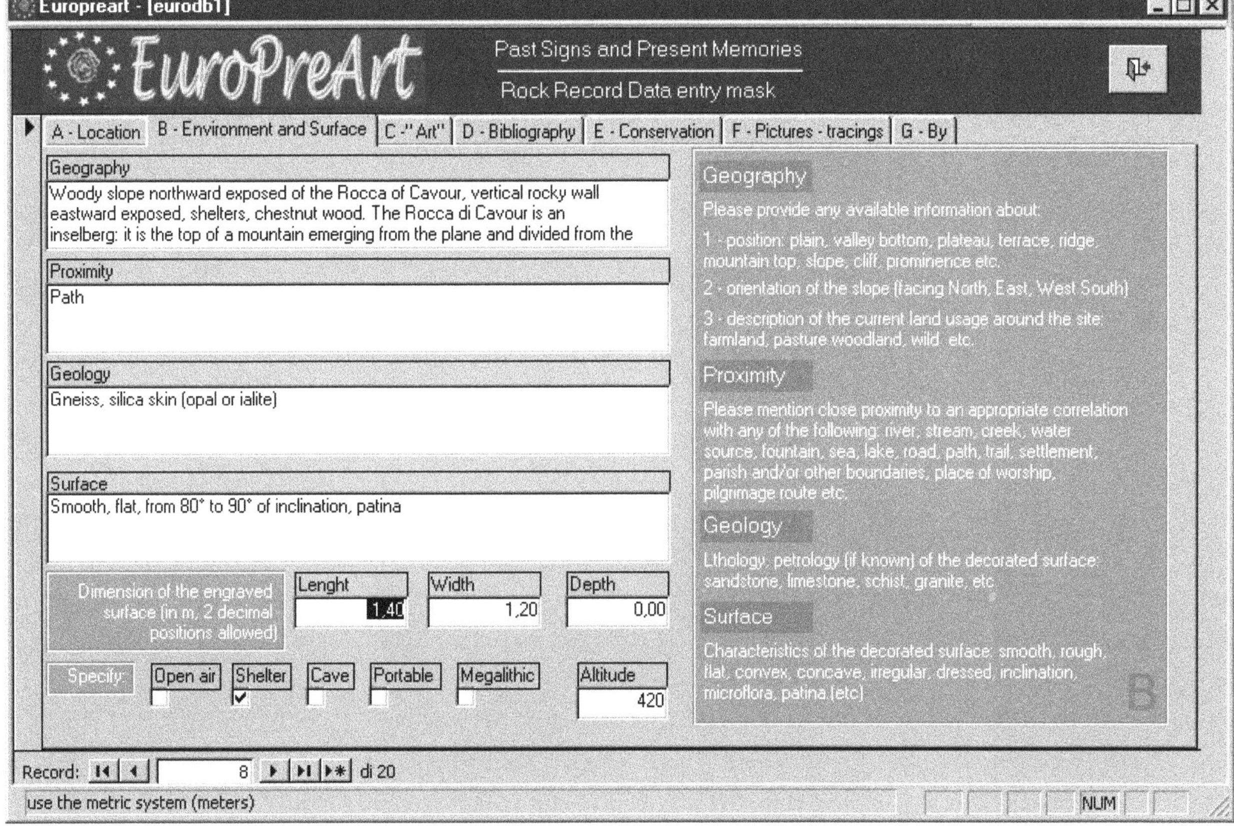

Fig. 4.2. Page B – Environment and Surface

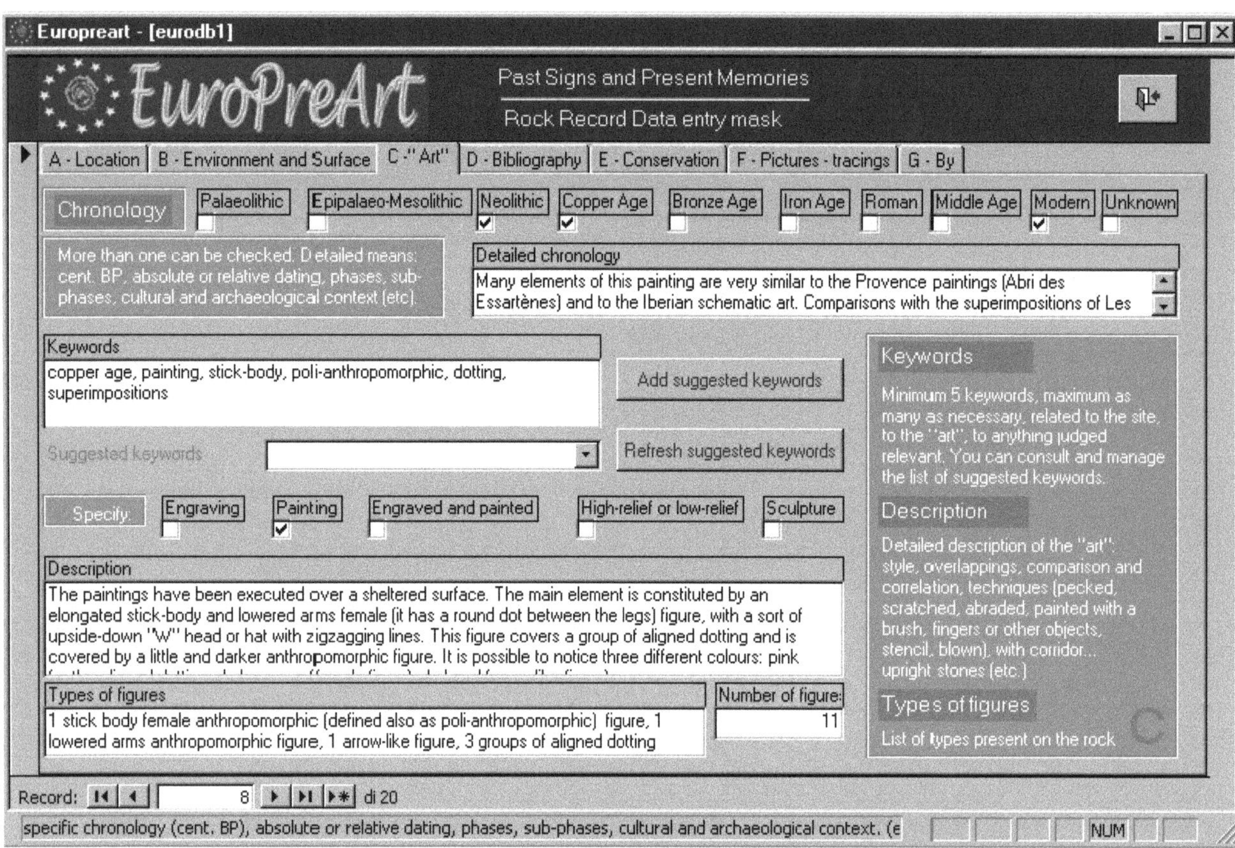

Fig. 4.3. Page C – "Art"

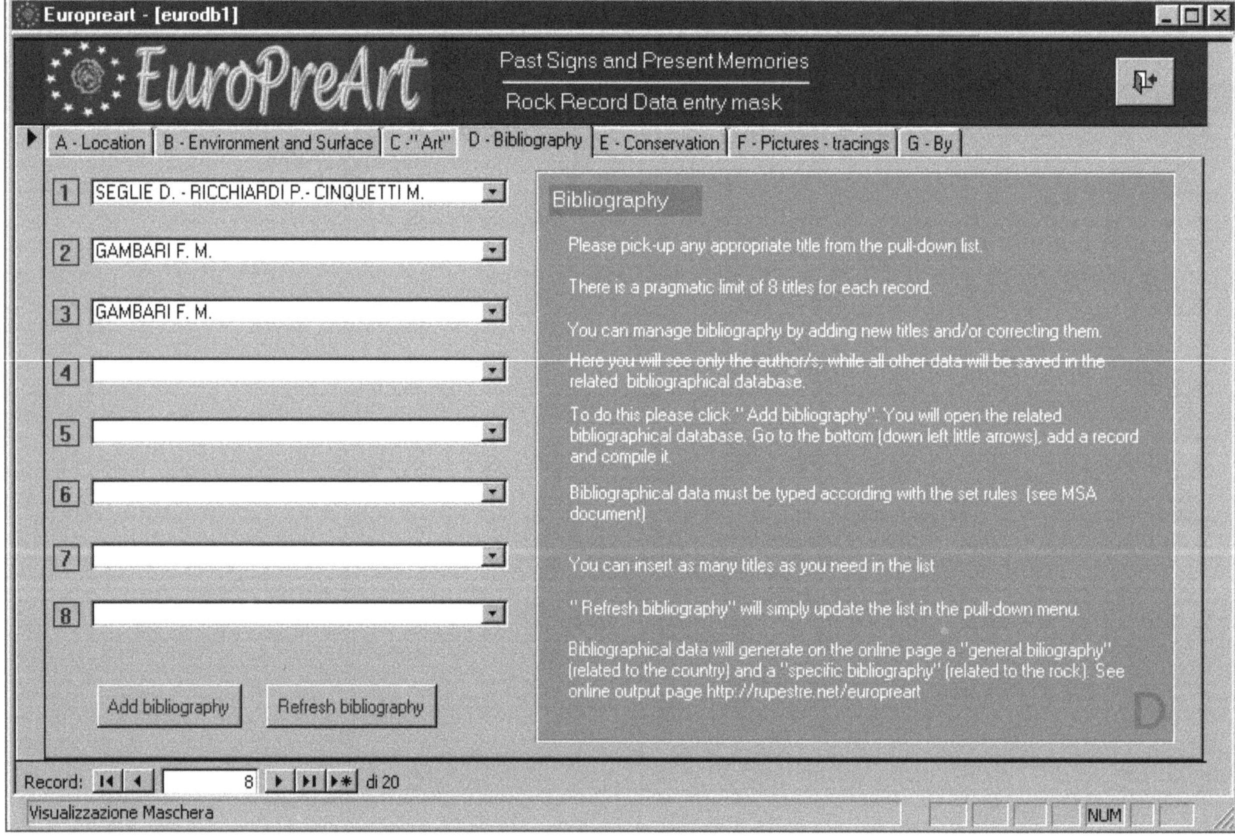

Fig. 4.4. Page D – Bibliography

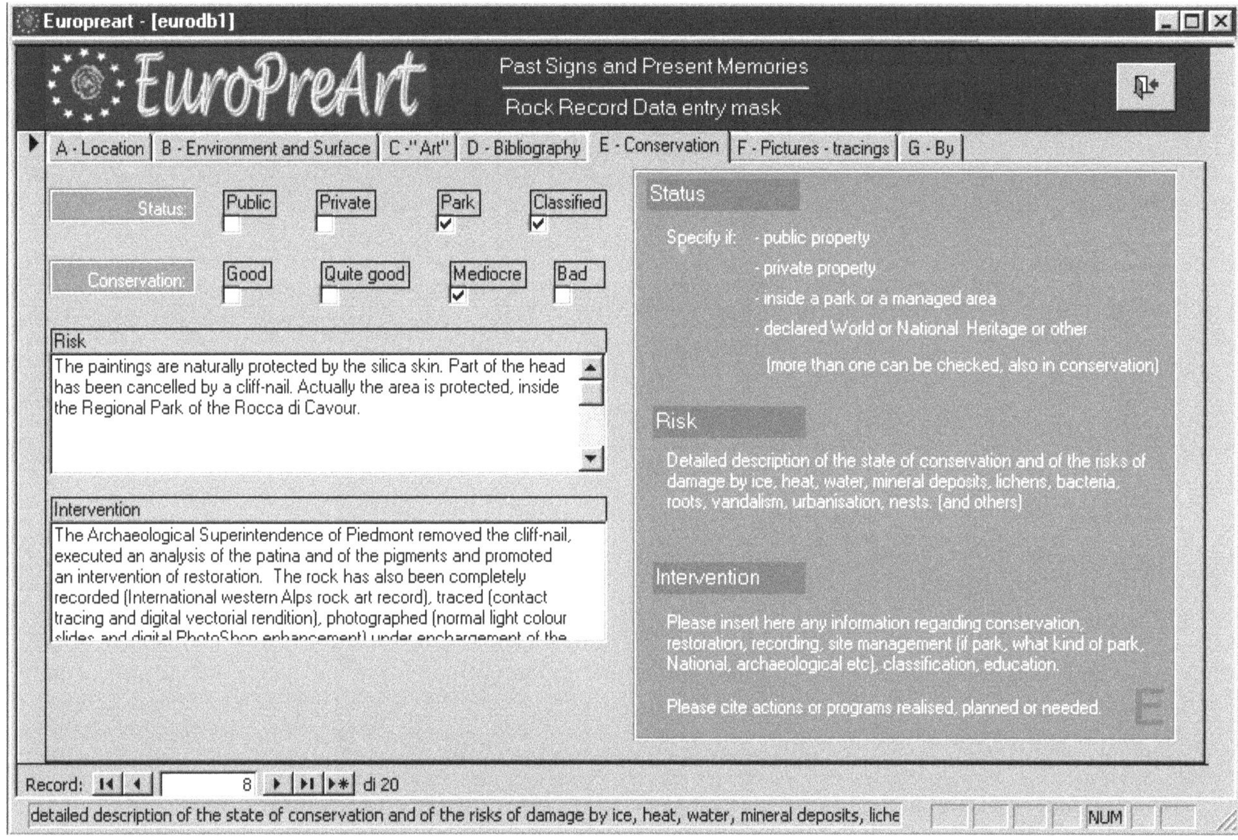

Fig. 4.5. Page E – Conservation

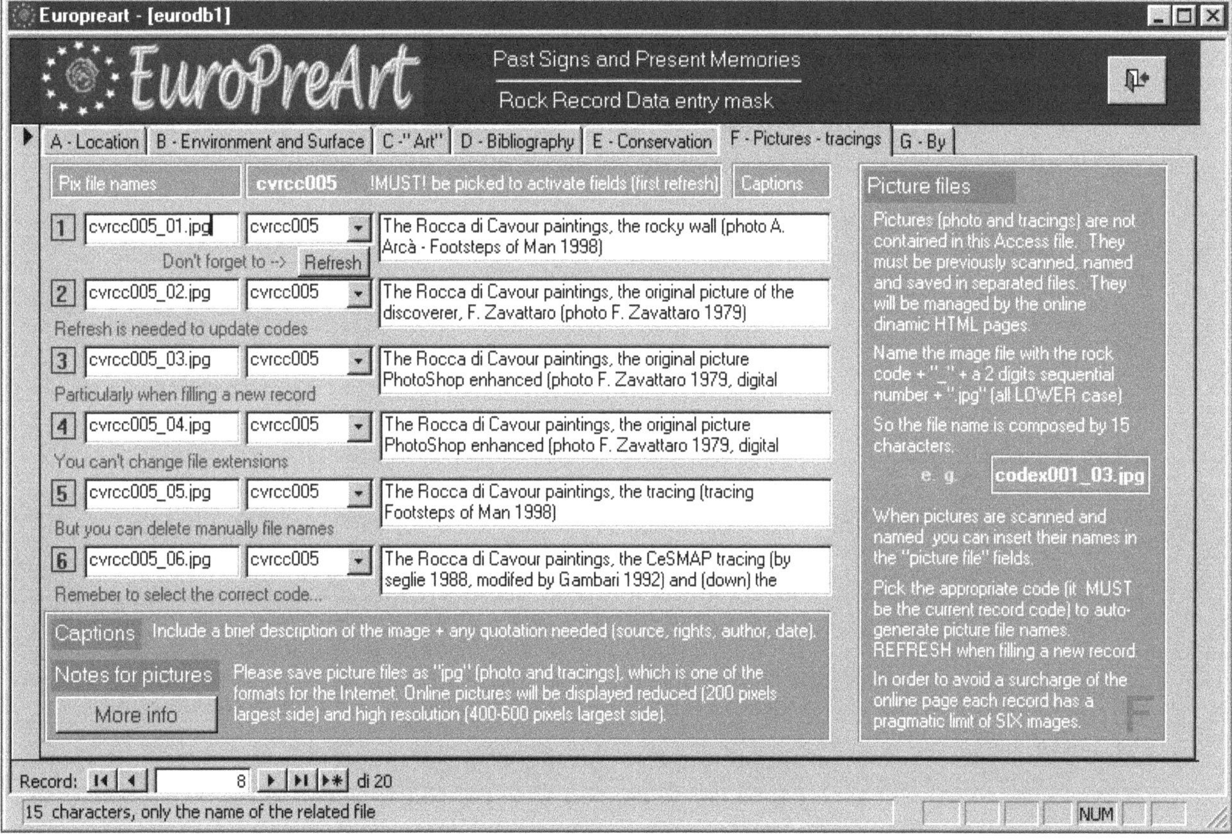

Fig. 4.6. Page F – Pictures – tracings

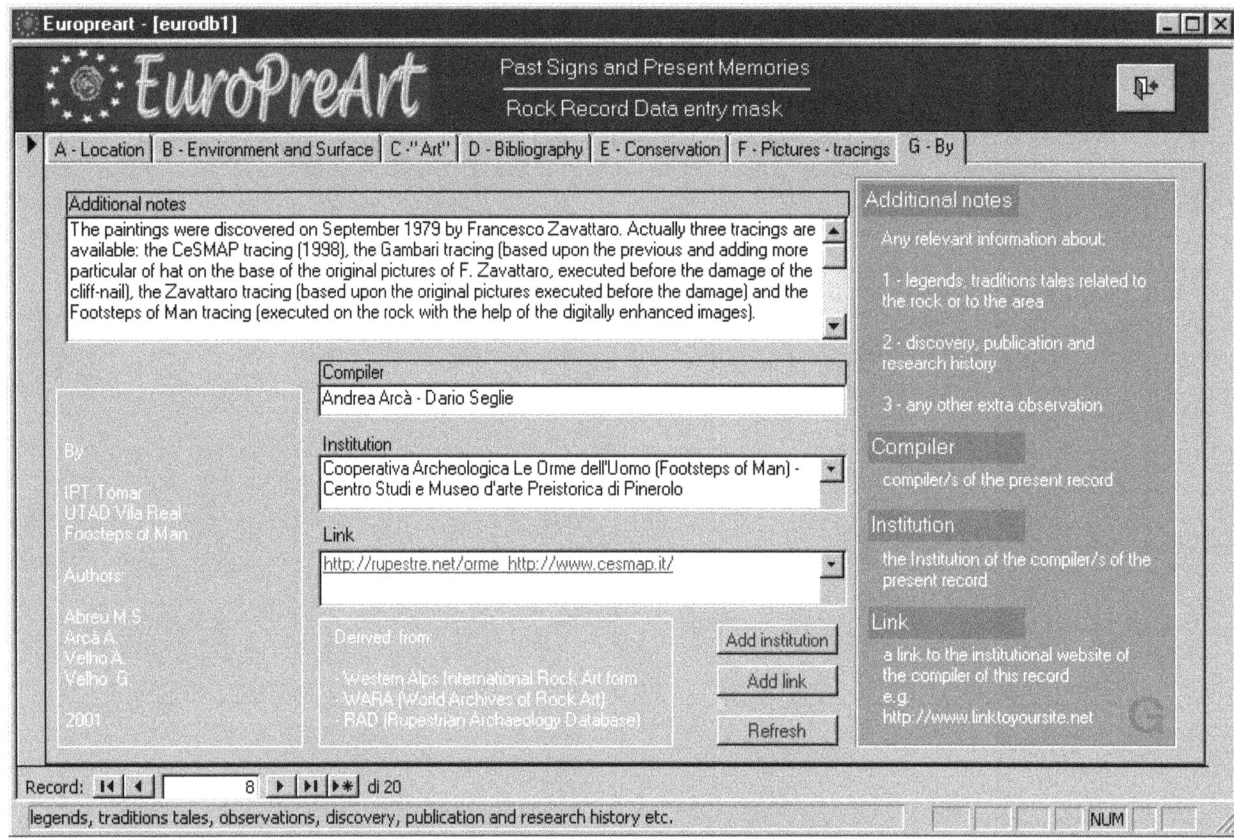

Fig. 4.7. Page G – By

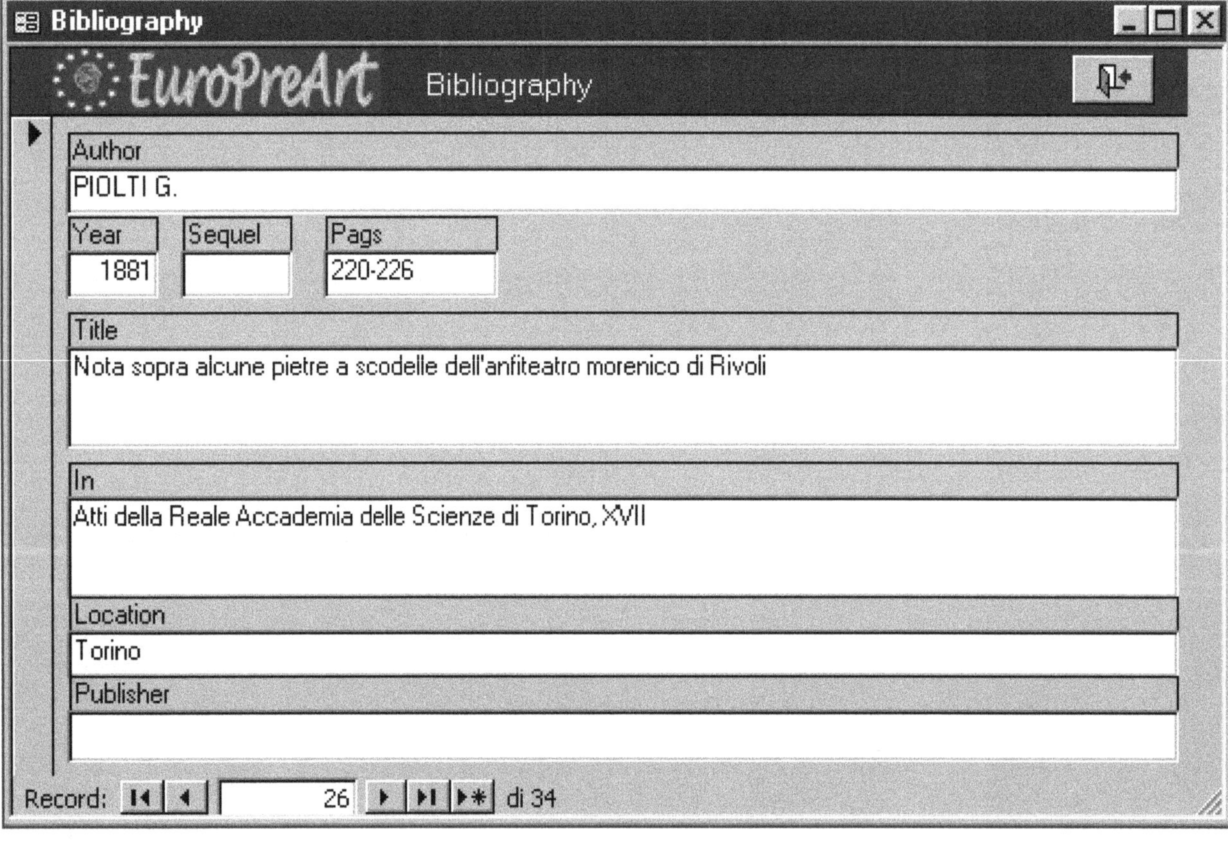

Fig. 4.8. Biblio

(www.baserunner.com), a shareware resource, provides the database capability of the EuroPreArt Web site (europreart.net). It runs under Linux or Windows servers.

The EuroPreArt Database System presents its results in the europreart.net site: seven European countries are involved (Denmark, France, Ireland, Italy, Portugal, Spain and Sweden), with more than 750 records of prehistoric art, 2000 images and 2500 reference titles. We hope that the project will be able to offer significant data to both general and specialist audiences. We hope also that future improvements will add new sets of records, widening the covered area and deepening the documentation capabilities, so achieving a complete sites-surfaces-figures structure.

Prehistoric art is part of the common heritage of all the people of the world, regardless of their social, cultural, religious or economic status. Often prehistoric art is the only record left by our human predecessors. It is the sole example, left in the landscape, of the intellectual capacities of our forefathers. It doesn't belong only to us and it is our duty to safeguard it for the generations to come. To study and to take care of any engraved or painted rock, cave, monument or object is essential to understanding and preserving it. The protection of the immediate surroundings must be part of any research effort.

Any prehistoric art researcher should respect local, national or international laws protecting archaeological sites and monuments. Rules, laws or requests of any individuals or organisations having legal or common rights must be taken in consideration. In the event of a conflict with the holders of the laws (e.g., a Government or authority that gives permission for the destruction of a prehistoric art site or object), a researcher should appeal to international organisations and entities dedicated to heritage protection (for example UNESCO, ICOMOS, IFRAO, etc). In case of planned or imminent destruction, a researcher should use all proper means, including legal mechanisms or civil rights action, to stop the destruction or damage of any prehistoric art site monument or object. A researcher should always remember that local people are key elements in the strategy of protecting and promoting a site or monument. Nothing in the recording, study or preservation processes should be made that could, even in the future, damage or prevent other actions or studies. In case of imminent destruction a careful review must establish all possible methods and techniques that can be used. A prehistoric art researcher should publish, present and be prepared to show and discuss his methodology, work and results to other colleagues or people interested. He must take great care to preserved the data, records and other relevant information. This is especially important in the case of a site, monument or object that was, or will be destroyed. Copies of all the records should always be made and kept in different locations.

Publication in scientific journals and presentation of results in scientific meetings should be encouraged. However, in the case of areas without proper controls, it important to take in consideration that any other kind of dissemination of information can be potentially dangerous for the art and even for the public. The copyright and ownership of the studies must clear, especially where public money was used. Appropriate references, acknowledgements or fees must always accompany the use of data, studies or images.

RECORDING

Recording is an essential part of the study of a prehistoric art area, monument or object. It is essentially for two main purposes: research and management. All recordings are incomplete. This is especially true if only one technique is used. A good "recording" should be an effort combining different techniques (e.g., photography, drawing and tracing). A multidisciplinary approach is best and should be used. Every case is unique and every element should be carefully studied.

Physical interference with the surface should be avoided, as far as this is possible. No substances should be applied to the rock surface. Methods like the Neutral Treatment (Anati's back and white) chalking or wetting painted or engraved surfaces have been abandoned by conscientious researchers. It was proved that they damage the art and the surface and in most cases, identical results can be obtained with other techniques. Less intrusive methods, like photography are advised. The use of proper lighting, mirrors and screens give good results in most of the cases. However, spotlights can be potentially dangerous if they are used inside caves and when the temperature gradients are relevant, or provoke the growth of algae and fungus. Tracing on plastic sheets can be made if the researcher arrives to the conclusion that it doesn't damage figures or surfaces. The recording process must not imply cleaning, scratching or removing any elements of the surface without proper studies and considerations. The advice of an expert in conservation is essential before any of the above actions take place. For example, when lichens are removed they will usually grow faster and stronger and if they are eliminated they cannot be use in the lichenometry. If a surface must be cleaned, it is necessary to leave at least half without any interference.

New methods like the use of laser-scanning should be proper investigated. There maybe unknown effects on painted and engraved surfaces. Moulds or other kind of three-dimensional copies should be avoid and only applied in presence of imminent destruction. The use of standard aids like the IFRAO scale or the Munsell soil colour scale should be used. Qualified people should make the recording. The researcher should teach his techniques. As in any archaeological work, people and jobs should be properly matched. A site facing imminent destruction should be recorded by a well-prepared and experienced team. There is usually no reason why a site should not be recorded more than once.

Above all, any methods use in recording should not interfere with other studies (e.g., dating, and conservation).

CONSERVATION

Conservation should be left in the hand of highly professional persons. Unfortunately not many exist that dedicate themselves to preservation of prehistoric art. A researcher should first of all try to understand the dynamics of the deterioration (why, when, by whom). Any conservation action should take in the consideration not only the immediate future but also beyond that. Any action should normally follow the recording and other research processes.

CONCLUSION

The extreme vulnerability of Prehistoric Art in conservation terms around the world is now widely acknowledged, not only by scholars but also by the educated general public. There is a growing understanding that we need to approach Rock Art management planning in as broadly based a way as possible: that is the way of principles of sustainable development in the field of Cultural Heritage preservation. We are now at the stage were we should re-assess each of our action, from the field work to the responsibility to disseminate knowledge through teaching and general educational programmes. These must be supported by our new professional code of conduct, and by a strengthened ethical approach.

References

SEGLIE, D. (ed). 2001. Prehistoric Art: Guide to Good Practice. EuroPreArt Project. Culture 2000 EU Programme, CeSMAP Editions, Pinerolo.

Web Site: http://europreart.net

PHILIPPI ROCK ART. GUIDELINES FOR A METHODOLOGICAL RECOVERY AND PREVENTIVE ACTION

George DIMITRIADIS
Hellenic Rock Art Centre, Philippi, GREECE, E-mail: giorgio.dimitriadis@cheapnet.it

Fernando COIMBRA
University of Salamanca, Salamanca, SPAIN, E-mail: facoimbra@yahoo.com

Carmelo PRESTIPINO
International Institute Ligurian Studies, Savona, Italy

***Abstract**: HERAC rock art documentation campaign focus its attention especially at the post-excavation and record process. We asked about finding destiny and which was the best temporary recovery action to undertake to protect properly the new archaeological data as came out from the rocky unearth and cliffs safeguard from vandalisms. We proceed to the rock cover by special membranes and smooth special sand mix respecting three basic conservation criteria: 1. to avoid humidity; 2. keep constant the temperature; 3. prohibit sunlight exposition. In fact all these parameters are mainly responsible for lichens and parasites affect and exfoliation, caused by the temperature variation between day and night, of the rocky surface.*
***Keywords**: Philippi rock art, Preventive Action, Archiviation and Data Management*

***Résumé**: Foyer de campagne de documentation d'art de roche de HERAC son attention particulièrement au processus d' poteau – excavation et de disque. Nous sommes enquis de trouver le destin et ce qui était la meilleure action provisoire de rétablissement à s'engager à se protéger correctement les nouvelles données archéologiques comme est venu dehors du rocheux déterre et de la sauvegarde de falaises des vandalismes. Nous procédons à la couverture de roche par les membranes spéciales et le mélange spécial doux de sable respectant trois critères de base de conservation: 1. pour éviter l'humidité; 2. constante de subsistance la température; 3. interdisez l'exposition de lumière du soleil. En fait tous ces paramètres sont principalement responsables des lichens et les parasites affectent et exfoliation, provoqué par la variation de la température entre jour et nuit, de la surface rocheuse.*
***Mots cles**: Action préventive, archiviation et gestion des data, rock art de Philippi*

INTRODUCTION

Most of the archaeological rock art evidence analysed so far refers to the transitional period between Late Bronze Age and Early Iron Age (Dimitriadis 2001). Following a founding research (DRP) by George Dimitriadis (1998-2000) and financed by the Municipality of Philippi, a joint cooperation between HERAC-IISL-ALA has been initiated in 2004 and the "Hellenic Rock Art Documentation Project" (HRAD) started a full investigation of the rock art in the area of Philippi. The project has been approved by the Greek Ministry of Culture and is financed by "Culture Enterprise" of the Municipality of Philippi and by the Ministry of Macedonia/Thrace.

CONTEXT

Geomorphologic Analysis

The area being investigated is located in East Macedonia. The geologic substratum is composed by granite, syenite, diorite and marble. During the Holocene the plain of Drama or plain of Philippi was characterized by marshes and alluvial depositions. Since the seventh millennium BC, the climate in the region remains stable and pollen and pedological analyses prove that the area was covered by wooden flora (Davidson-Thomas 1986).

The HRAD research area is delimited by Mt. Phalakro (2111 m.) and Mt. Orvilos (1888 m.) to the north; Mt. Pangaion (1965 m.) and the Philippi Marshes (now drained) to the southwest; and Mt. Symbolo (694 m.) to the southeast.

The Rock Art Sites

Rock art sites of prophet Helias (πρ. Ηλίας Φ/Β.1-1α, 1β, Β.2, Β.3-Eiv) and Mana (Μάνα Φ/Β.1, Β.2, Β.3, Β.4-Eiv) are located in the Municipality of Philippi, parish of Filippoi in Kavala Province. (Figure 5.1, Aerial Photograph). The GPS coordinates are: prophet Helias (πρ.Ηλίας Φ/Β.2): 41° 01'676" N / 24° 01'822" E / elevation: 189 +/- 7 m. and Mana (Μάνα Φ/Β.1): 41°01'794" N / 24°20'999" E / elevation: 238 +/- 5 m.

Methodology of Documentation

Phase I (DRP)

The fieldwork was carried out in three years and focussed on the area of prophet Helias. A survey of the area was carried out to record essential environmental data and signs of ancient anthropic activity. Gallery mines for the extraction of iron mineral were in use until the 18th century and probably were already in use in antiquity. Surface cleaning was carried out according to the neutral method (Anati 1977); the state of conservation of the engraved rocks determined. The engravings have been recorded by frottage technique (the high roughness of the surfaces has caused unsatisfactory results) and tracing on PVC standard sheets (90x1.20 cm) where applicable.

Phase II (HRAD)

In the second phase, the hypothesis proposed by Dimitriadis (1999b) about the possibility that the prophet Helias area was an open air sanctuary of the Hedones has been tested. Exposing more surface of the known engraved rocks and completing the tracing on sheets of all carved rocks has revealed more carvings. New discoveries characterize this phase (publication forthcoming) and we were able to determine better the dating frame of cupules (Dimitriadis 2005b).

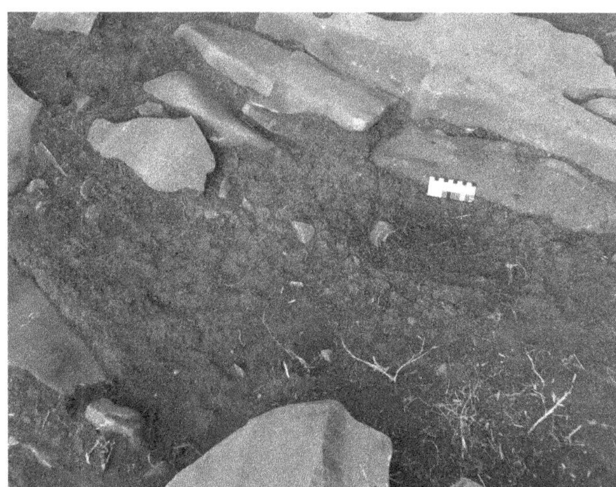

Fig. 5.1. Rock: πρ.Ηλίας Φ/Β.1. Philippi. Archaeological level where the pit hole is located. Photo before remove darkish material. © Photo HERAC54

Photogrammetric survey of rocky surface

During the 2006 fieldwork season Ida Mailland (ALA, Archaeological Association of Lombardy, Milan-Italy), Davide Delfino (IISL, International Institute Ligurian Studies, Savona-Italy) and Andrea Vianello (University of Sheffield) have attempted a photogrammetric and GIS survey of the rocks. GIS software packages are also being used. A fixed frame (0.60x 0.80 m) has been used as reference after the impossibility to use specialist equipment due to the uneven nature of the terrain. Particular care has been taken to maintain the carvings under adequate natural light; the photographs have been therefore taken in batches during a week. The resulting photographs will require substantial post-processing and are intended to become a tool of research and experimentation to further the study of carvings in their original context.

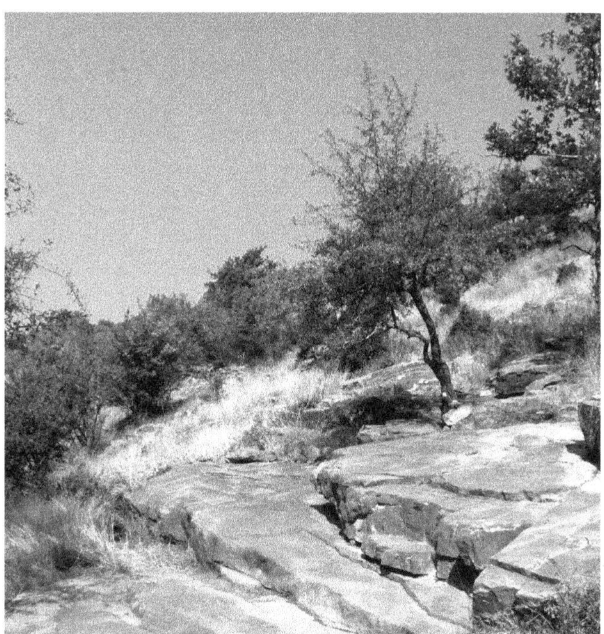

Fig. 5.2. Rock: Μάνα Φ/Β.1. Philippi. The rocky surface is located nearby a seasonal water stream. © Photo HERAC

Recovery and Preventive Action during both phases

HERAC rock art documentation campaign focus its attention especially at the post-excavation and record process. We asked about finding destiny and which was the best temporary recovery action to undertake in order to protect properly the new archaeological data as came out from the rocky unearth and cliffs safeguard from vandalisms.

During the accurate cleaning and stratigraphic exploration of the area πρ.Ηλίας Φ/Β1, a pit hole full of darkish terrain was unearthed. Carmelo Prestipino has determined in laboratory the presence of charcoal in the terrain [Figure 5.1]. The geomorpology of rock Μάνα Φ/Β.1 is under study by Daniela Cardoso (Museum Martins Sarmento-Portugal) in order to establish the conservation action to be undertaken in the future [Figure 5.2].

After an attend examination of the natural and human hazardous situation document by Dimitriadis (2006) the team proceed to the rock cover πρ.Ηλίας Φ/Β1, B2 & B3 by special membranes for and smooth special sand mix. Different materials were taken in consideration under the technical supervisor of a restoration expert, Mr. Michael Karavelides (HERAC). The choice was directed in a special multi-strata material which can resist in high and low temperatures and respecting three basic conservation criteria: 1. to avoid humidity; 2. keep constant the temperature; 3. prohibit sunlight exposition. In fact all these parameters are mainly responsible for lichens and parasites affect and exfoliation, caused by the temperature variation between day and night, of the rocky surface. In particular a small protuberance of rock Φ/B1 remains uncovers just to determine, after one year atmospheric agents exposition, the condition of the rocky surface [Figure 5.3].

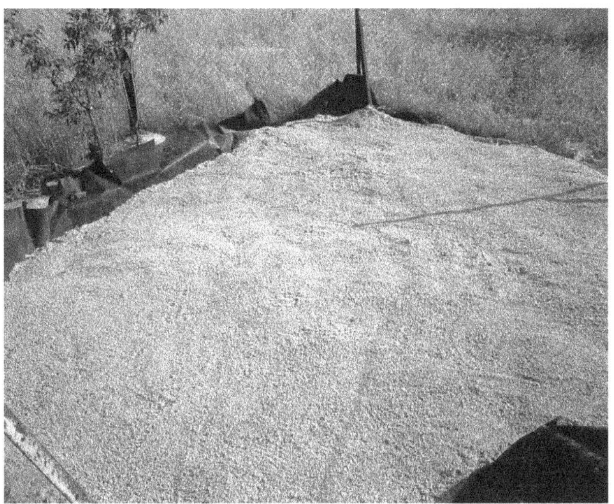

Fig. 5.3. Rock: πρ.Ηλίας Φ/Β.1. A thick stratum of special material covers special tick *folio*. Action undertaken in the end of the fieldwork (August 2005). © Photo HERAC

Technical Data

Indeed, the *folio* [Figure 5.4] as reproduced in Technical Data Schedule [Table 5.1] guarantee, despite the temporary of the recover action, an all weather protection and functionality during the phase of re-opening of the site for further studies. A quantity of 6 tons of special sand and ~60 m² *folio* used for covering all three rocky surfaces located in prophet Helias site.

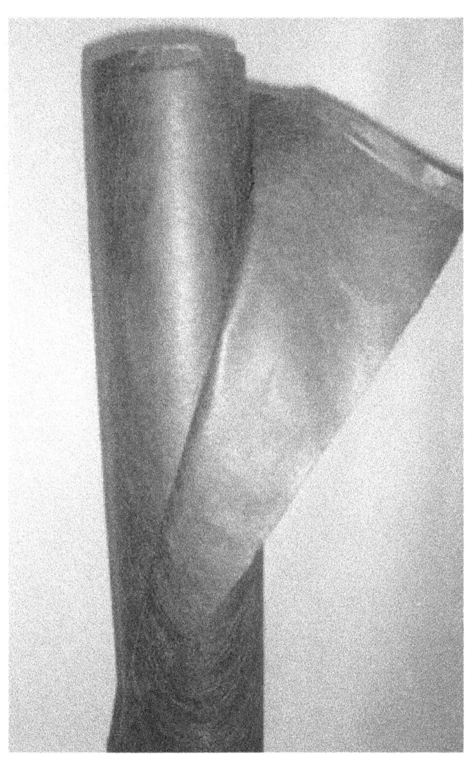

Fig. 5.4. Vimat-Bit *folio*. A quantity of ~60m^2 *folio* was used for covering all three rocks located in prophet Helias area. © Photo VIMATEC Inc.

Tab. 5.1. Technical Table Vimat-Bit sheet

Characteristics	Norm	Value	Unit of measure
Weight	EN 1849-1	380±5%	g/m^2
Thickness	EN 1849-1	0,6±15%	Mm
Tensile Strength	EN 12311-1	Long: 300±15% Trans: 280±15%	N/5
Elongation	EN 12311-1	Long: 40% Trans: 50%	%
Nail Tearing	EN 12310-1	Long: 150±15% Trans: 150±15%	N
Water Vapour Permeabilitv	DIN 52615	WDD = 1,1 μ = 37599 Sd = 24,06	g/m^{2}x24h m
Water Impermeability	EN 20811	≥3	MH$_2$O
Static Punching	U.E.A.t.c. (5.1.9)		

Acknowledgments

HERAC staff and all the team warmly thanks the Major of Philippi Mr. Kotaides for the immediate financial efforts and technical supports needed for the recovery and prevention campaign. Special thanks are also reserved to the VIMATEC Inc., Thessalonica-Greece for the timeliness to provide all the necessary material and it's gently concession to publish commercial material.

References

ANATI, E. 1977. Methods of Recording and Analysing Rock Engravings. *Studi Camuni*, Vol. 7: 64.

DAVIDSON, D.A., THOMAS, B. 1986. Geomorphological Studies in Collin Renfrew *et al.* (ed.), *Excavations at Sitagroi. A Prehistoric Village in Northeastearn Greece*, Monumenta Archaeologica 13, 1: 25-40. Los Angeles, University of California.

DIMITRIADIS, G. 2001. Arte Rupestre Mediterranéo: el ejemplo del arte rupestre helénico, BARA (4): 143-152.

DIMITRIADIS, G. 2005. Hellenic Rock Art. Cupmarks Configurations and Patterns. IV Annual Schematic Rock Art Workshop, Saviore dell'Adamello-Valcamonica, Italy.

DIMITRIADIS, G. 2006. Assessing Natural and Anthropic Hazards on Greek Rock Art. *ARKEOS* (16): 45-62.

COIMBRA, F. (in press). When open air carved rocks become sanctuaries: methodological criteria for a classification. Proceedings of the XV UISPP Congress.

INVENTARIOS GRÁFICOS Y GEOGRÁFICOS: UN PROYECTO DE REGISTRO Y CONSERVACIÓN DEL ARTE RUPESTRE EN COLOMBIA

Guillermo MUÑOZ

Director of Indigenous Rock Art Research Group, GIPRI-Colombia, Cra 57 No.174-12, Bogotá, COLOMBIA, E-mail: gipricolombia@gmail.com

Judith TRUJILLO

Research of Indigenous Rock Art Research Group, GIPRI-Colombia, Calle 63 No. 73a-31, A. 702ª Bogotá, COLOMBIA, E-mail: judithtt@gmail.com

Abstract: *From the same beginning of the investigations the team of GIPRI built a group of formats that they were being developed slowly (1970-1990-2005). The quality of these materials has improved significantly with the development of the programs of digital manipulation as of the organization of geographical systems of information. The old databases (Access), the materials of diverse sources and activities have not had difficulty to adapt to the new technologies, to have been formulated with Cartesian systems from the same beginning of the investigation. In 1996-98 it was carried out a work that sought to unify all the materials and to generate a model to document the rock art in Colombia. The developments of this thematic has had in the last years (2000-2005) will help to observe in the complex group of file systems and formats in which incorporate graphic and photographically: the locations, the evaluation about the alteration conditions and agents of deterioration, etc. The systematizing of these elements in the programs of geographical information allows having new sources, to determine more concrete ways to the conservation and administration of the rupestrian places.*

Keywords: *Rock art, Recording, Documentation, Conservation, Geographic Information Systems*

Résumé: *Du même commencement des enquêtes l'équipe de GIPRI a construit un groupe de formats qu'ils étaient développés lentement (1970-1990-2005). La qualité de ces matières a amélioré considérablement avec le développement des programmes de manipulation numérique (systèmes d'information géographique). Les bases de données anciennes (Accès), les matières de sources diverses et activités n'ont pas eu de difficulté de s'adapter aux nouvelles technologies, ayant été formulé avec les systèmes Cartésiens du même commencement de l'enquête. En 1996-98 il a été porté dehors un travail qui a cherché á unifier toutes les matières et produire un modèle pour documenter l'art Rupestre en Colombie. Les développements de ce thématique a eu dans les dernières années (2000-2005) aidera pour observer dans le complexe groupe de systèmes du dossier et formats dans lequel incorpore graphiquement et photographiquement: les emplacements, l'évaluation au sujet de la modification des conditions et les agents de détérioration, etc. Le réduire ces éléments dans ces programmes de systèmes d'information géographique autorise d'avoir de nouvelles sources, déterminées chemins plus concrets à la conservation et administration des places rupestres.*

Mots clefs: *Art Rupestre, Enregistrement, Documentation, Conservation, Systèmes Géographiques d'information*

La discusión que aquí se esboza pretende solamente discutir algunos aspectos relativos al sistema complejo de documentación, dejando para otra oportunidad las implicaciones de estos documentos en las peculiaridades del estudio del sentido cultural, del pensamiento y el lenguaje de las representaciones rupestres precolombinas en Colombia.

INTRODUCCIÓN

Hace algunos años, quienes trabajaban en arte rupestre en Colombia tenían fundamentalmente la preocupación de producir documentos que facilitaran sin mucha prevención el despliegue de sus interpretaciones (Ancizar, 1850). Eran realmente muy pocos los grupos o personas que al investigar la estética precolombina, el arte de estas culturas y con ello, los murales rupestres, entendieran la necesidad de realizar un registro sistemático y riguroso de las diversas particularidades de los sitios rupestres que estudiaban.

Cuando se iniciaron las exploraciones, los primeros registros, en los mismos sitios donde trabajaron los autores clásicos en el altiplano cundiboyacense en Colombia (Isaacs J.-(1885) publicado 1967; Triana, 1922; Cabrera Ortiz- (1942) publicado 1972), de inmediato fue posible poder percibir un conjunto interesante y problemático de inconsistencias. No solamente se constató que las interpretaciones eran apresuradas, sino que se pudo confirmar en cada caso, que aquellos mínimos registros en algunas zonas del altiplano, se apresuraban a resaltar ciertos trazos o elementos de los murales, privilegiando algunos "temas", y excluían aspectos que muy seguramente pudieran entorpecer la versión general de sus teorías. Es evidente que los vínculos que estos autores hacían entre los motivos rupestres y sus interpretaciones estaban basados en inadecuadas formas de registro, en estructuras teóricas, aún no desarrolladas o mal digeridas, con lo cual se generó en cada caso, una imagen falsa o por lo menos distorsionada en relación a los sistemas de representación y lo que es más grave, se produjo una explicación de la presencia de los habitantes precolombinos, que bajo estas interpretaciones y registros, se veía como si fuera primitivo e in-esencial. No se entendió la complejidad de estos sistemas de representación y todos y cada uno de los elementos simbólicos que dejaron estas etnias en el territorio, con un conjunto amplísimo de zonas con pinturas y grabados, un lenguaje y un pensamiento peculiar y complejo, fueron mirados como algo simplemente infantil.

Así que lo que parece más evidente cuando se estudia la historia de la investigación (Gipri 1985-2004) es que los diversos autores, según el espíritu de la época, sus conocimientos, e intereses, resuelven dar fácilmente un sentido y una explicación a los trazos pintados o grabados precolombinos, sin que tenga especial importancia los trazos mismos, y si estos sean o no realmente como se encuentran en la roca *in situ*. Diversas versiones de un mismo mural y casi siempre incompleto, constituye un conjunto de materiales dispersos de distintas publicaciones, de diferentes épocas, en donde todas las versiones están realmente muy alejadas de las particularidades de su forma, composición y proporción. Esto es lo más característico del modo tradicional como se han venido denunciando y describiendo los sitios rupestres.

Esta variedad de referencias ha permitido realizar algunas reflexiones sobre el estudio de la historia de los registros y la complejidad del tema y lo que es más importante generar algunas propuestas de trabajo hacia el futuro, no sólo en lo relativo a la consecución y manejo de las fuentes documentales, a los problemas teóricos y prácticos del registro, sino a los posibles caminos que vinculan al arte y la arqueología, al aporte que puede dar la discusión filosófica y sus vínculos históricos con la ciencia.

Lo interesante es que al reflexionar sobre la diversidad de dichos materiales, al detenerse en sus relaciones y diferencias, es posible entender que en una muy buena parte de estos **documentos tradicionales no se encuentran ubicados en un modelo moderno de descripción**. Cuando se estudian en detalle los temas que trabajaron los autores que realizaron tales trabajos y se observan las primeras transcripciones, es posible constatar que no sólo no existía una formación moderna, que permitiera una documentación con ciertos niveles de fidelidad, sino que tampoco existían para la época elementos teóricos y **fundamentos científicos en el ámbito arqueológico**, que permitieran ordenar con criterio universal la complejidad de preguntas, que orienten el sentido del registro y el grado y nivel de resolución de los documentos y mucho menos, los refinamientos teóricos que ahora son posibles para fundamentar el modo de hacer las descripciones, según lo que busca explicar el investigador. Diversas preguntas sobre el proceso metodológico se fueron estructurando y con ellas inquietudes sobre el modo de realizar las diversas modalidades de registro, en el ámbito nacional e internacional. No sólo era importante realizar registros con calidad gráfica y fotográfica, introducir en la descripción las cartografías para determinar el lugar de los yacimientos rupestres, sino que era indispensable entender las razones, por las cuales estos procedimientos fundamentados teóricamente, eventualmente conducirían al conocimiento de las representaciones rupestres, a determinar sus peculiaridades y con ellas, a hacer mas comprensibles algunos niveles de la cultura, es decir de los sistemas intelectuales de representación presentes en el lenguaje precolombino.

El sentido de todo lo que debería hacerse debería estar orientado a dar cuenta de la relación entre las obras rupestres y los grupos que habitaron el territorio. Las preocupaciones sobre cómo describir "los temas" rupestres y la manera de realizar el estudio de los motivos y a la descripción de los mismos se hace más compleja cuando se entiende que existen problemas teóricos que están implícitos en los trabajos, aún en las actividades mas elementales. ¿Son ahora los sistemas de registro del arte rupestre realmente, por refinados que parezcan estructuras modernas? ¿Qué tipo de condiciones deberán tener para que se aproximen aunque sea a las formas de trabajo convencionales de las ciencias afines?

LA POLÉMICA Y SUS CONSECUENCIAS

> *"Las ciencias empíricas son sistemas de teorías; y la lógica del conocimiento científico, por tanto, puede describirse como una teoría de teorías" (Popper, Karl. La Lógica de la Investigación Científica.* Primera Edición Rel. Méjico. 1991. pp. 57-74)

Si imaginamos un sistema absolutamente contrario, un sistema ideal, totalmente opuesto al descrito anteriormente, tendríamos muy seguramente uno que se interesa en registrar todas y cada una de las particularidades y con ello, los singulares detalles del mural, e imaginar que se está haciendo un trabajo riguroso y meticuloso de registro. ¿Cual sería, según esta versión ideal, el grado de resolución que tendría que tener la documentación que debería efectuarse? ¿Hasta qué límite es posible llegar a describir los diversos eventos? ¿Qué es lo que resulta ser finalmente significativo? ¿Son las ciencias básicas las que determinan el grado y la clase de información, o están muchas mas cosas en juego? La descripción infinita de aspectos, la búsqueda de detalles, la adecuación de procedimientos, el manejo de equipos y técnicas, que permitan observar singularidades diversas, parecería ser la ruta de los trabajos científicos en arte rupestre y sin embargo, es indispensable comprender que este camino nunca ha sido el que aproxima al desarrollo científico, por lo menos en occidente. Es necesario entonces reflexionar sobre estos procedimientos con cuidado y detenerse en los fundamentos teóricos que permitirían por lo menos acceder a ciertas rutas que orienten la búsqueda ahora desde una perspectiva moderna.

Es interesante reflexionar hasta dónde esta propuesta metodológica ideal está ubicada en las formas modernas de registro, es decir en el ámbito en que fue pensada la estructura fundamental de la ciencia, que se inaugura en el siglo XVI y con ella, un sistema de percepción que constituye la base de los modelos científicos. La modernidad se entiende como un período humano, que se ocupa en producir un sistema de percepción, un modelo matemático de topología, es decir una forma de ubicar los objetos en el espacio, determinando de esta forma su condición geográfica y generando una matemática de descripción (x, y).

No es completamente cierto entonces que la búsqueda de los detalles y singularidades y el registro de estos, sea una percepción moderna. Moderna es la escogencia de una estructura matemática para hacer con ella posible la experiencia. Así la construcción del objeto no es simplemente la atención a las singularidades de las cosas del mundo y que con ello sea inmediatamente posible garantizar la objetividad, al imitar los detalles de las cosas.

Cuando se asume una iniciativa que se ocupa de la historia, el proceso y las implicaciones teóricas del registro y sus vínculos con la teoría y las pretensiones de la interpretación, aparecen diversos caminos de nuevas preguntas que sin duda configuran un cuerpo complejo de niveles y problemas de la construcción del objeto de investigación. Algunas preguntas fueron formuladas en los comienzos mismos de la investigación y con ellas se fueron estructurando diversos desarrollos temáticos relativos al estado, las características de los sitios, las estructuras de los motivos, entre otros.

El camino inevitable para poder manejar una información útil, es poder considerar desde en comienzo mismo de las actividades ciertas formas de realizar los documentos, con niveles altos de refinamiento en las labores de registro. El propósito no es otro que el de producir documentos de diversa naturaleza, que se sostengan con cierta calidad en el tiempo, cabe decir que sean de tal forma estables por su condición, por su perspectiva científica, que puedan prolongarse aún con ciertos cambios tecnológicos, pues estos no alteran su condición fundamental. Solamente los materiales que tengan ciertas propiedades en la descripción podrán sobrevivir a este proceso y fácilmente se ubicarán en una compleja red de características que poseen los objetos que se pretenden estudiar. Sólo es posible esta transición cuando los sistemas de registro y documentación general están organizados en estructuras universales de descripción.

EL PROCESO Y LA EXPERIENCIA DE GIPRI

> *"Las teorías son redes que lanzamos para apresar aquello que llamamos "el mundo": para racionalizarlo, explicarlo y dominarlo. Y tratamos de que la malla sea cada vez más fina." (Popper, Karl. La Lógica de la Investigación Científica.* Primera Edición Rel. Méjico. 1991 *pp. 57-74)*

Cuando se iniciaron los trabajos de registro del arte rupestre en el altiplano Cundiboyacense en Colombia era necesario resolver, en primer lugar, temas de la tradición de los registros (Triana 1922, Cabrera Ortiz 1942-72), temas que fueron configurando poco a poco el sistema complejo que ahora GIPRI realiza de un modo riguroso. En primer lugar en el siglo XIX y comienzos del XX no existían criterios claros para realizar la descripción de los motivos rupestres, lo cual quiere decir que el dibujante descuidaba en cada caso la proporción y las formas de los trazos presentes en pinturas y grabados (Ancizar, M. y Comisión Corográfica 1850) generando así un levantamiento con muchas deficiencias. Un segundo aspecto lo constituía la dificultad de poder ubicar los sitios donde se encontraban las pinturas, pues los autores clásicos, descuidaban normalmente hacer una descripción gráfica de los lugares, limitándose únicamente a dar eventualmente alguna información de los sitios, normalmente como parte de un texto. Al igual que otras zonas del mundo, también estos autores escogían algunos temas y determinaban caprichosamente incluir la totalidad de los grupos pictóricos, describiendo y no siempre en detalle, los signos o aspectos que les llamaba la atención.

Hoy ya no es posible desconocer la complejidad que en el siglo XIX y en los primeros años del siglo XX los investigadores pasaban por alto. El propósito último de todos los trabajos de investigación y de todas las etapas ha sido la búsqueda sin duda de un refinamiento documental, que no debe entenderse como la simple recolección de datos sin dirección ni perspectiva. Al entender esta dinámica histórica el proyecto de investigación que se inicio en los años setenta, siempre estuvo interesado en construir una estructura coherente de información cualificada, derivada del trabajo de campo, y de las diversas fuentes existentes historia de la investigación. Lo esencial es que los documentos tengan la mejor calidad y con ella puedan ser útiles al ser considerados como materia prima para ser usada en diversos ambientes espacios de la investigación. Los registros colectados desde cierta perspectiva, serán objeto de las reflexiones sobre su sentido y función cultural pero también y como asunto complementario como documentos con alta resolución, que darán posibilidades al estudio del estado de los yacimientos, de la mano de las ciencias básicas.

El conjunto de preguntas de investigación que se realizan hacia una dirección y otra, serán sin duda vías para determinar el lenguaje y pensamiento de las representaciones, pero también para caracterizar los diversos asuntos concernientes al deterioro, sistemas de ejecución y las características bioclimáticas de los sitios. Sin estos aspectos será muy complicado establecer alguna dinámica futura de administración de los sitios rupestres. Pero para llegar a este aspecto fundamental el equipo tuvo que iniciar su trabajo desde aspectos menos complejos, más sencillos.

Desde el inicio el equipo consideró que era indispensable dimensionar las figuras, determinar los grupos pictóricos, reseñar los motivos y usar una expresión del dibujante, que permitiera con una escala apropiada tener acceso a

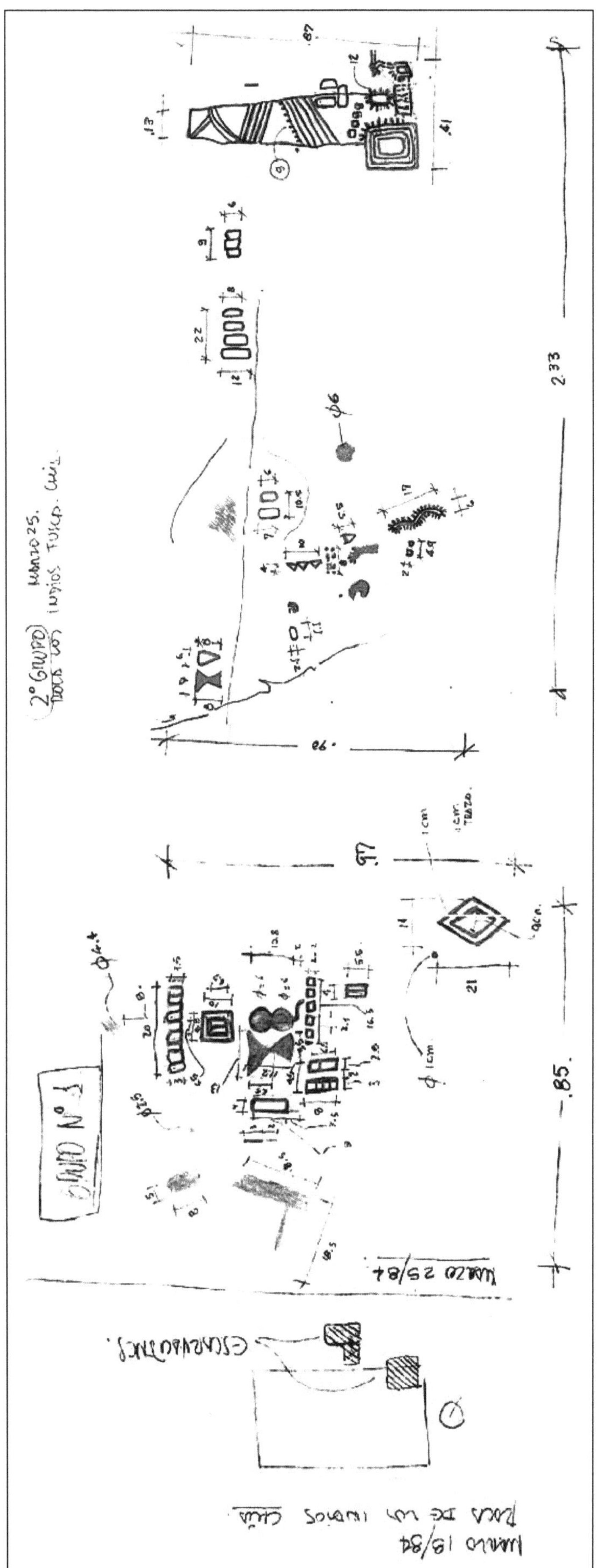

Fig. 6.1. *Historia de los sistemas de registro*. Dibujos Ricardo Muñoz. Desde los primeros formatos de registro Gipri se interesó por mostrar con gran detalle las formas de los dibujos, la posición exacta de los mismos dentro del mural y los estados de alteración en que se encontraban las pinturas. Aquí se muestra la trascripción de la Roca de Fusca, Chía, 1985

algunos de los detalles, incluso de aquellos que la versión fotográfica no permitía observar. El propósito central de esta época era poder reconstruir la estructura de los motivos rupestres con un alto grado de detalle (Figura 6.1). En esta misma época se iniciaron las bases de datos que incluían diversos temas de los registros, al igual que una memoria (formato) sobre el tipo de fotografía que se hacia de los sitios, de los murales y de los motivos rupestres con la discriminación de las diversas imágenes que se querían registrar. Se describían en estas fichas no solamente las condiciones técnicas de la película, de la cámara, sino también las características de la luz, y las condiciones de las diversas tomas, con el propósito fundamental de reconstruir las diversas condiciones en las que se encontraban los yacimientos rupestres y evaluar la calidad de los materiales.

En este proceso de construcción de un modelo, de una estructura metodológica para describir los sitios rupestres se organizaron las primeras fichas que permitieran describir con cierto detalle la situación de la roca o rocas y los sitios exactos en los cuales aparecían los conjuntos pictóricos. Una visión cartesiana para describir los objetos fue desde sus orígenes la formulación implícita, que le fue dando estructura a los diversos niveles y desarrollo de las fichas, que poco a poco se fueron transformando hasta la versión final de los últimos años (1975- 1980- 1990 2006). Al lado de estas descripciones relativamente complejas de las rocas, de sus caras y la descripción de los grupos y motivos pictóricos fue indispensable desarrollar adicionalmente su descripción cartográfica, eventualmente usando las planchas del gobierno (IGAC) o realizando algunas cartografías para dar mayor definición a los sitios cuando esto lo requería

Concientes de la historia de las descripciones se fue construyendo un sistema de registro, que no sólo pretendía incluir en los documentos los dibujos y formas representadas, sino también la forma del yacimiento y describir sus alrededores, como sus condiciones generales (Figuras 6.2 y 6.3). El proyecto era construir un sistema de información que integrara diversas condiciones de los sitios rupestres, con el cual los investigadores tuvieran una imagen completa y compleja de elementos. Las fichas de registro fueron poco a poco discriminando posibilidades de describir la estructura del territorio, el área, el entorno, del sitio preciso donde está la roca o el abrigo y con estas distinciones, se fueron organizando temas de trabajo que permitían aumentar los niveles de resolución para buscar describir el pigmento, el surco, los deterioros, las formas imperceptibles según la escala, pero ubicadas en unas cuadrículas, que con facilidad permitieran determinar con precisión los lugares dentro del mural, el grupo pictórico, allí donde se encuentran los elementos que por alguna razón resultan importantes de resaltar o privilegiar.

El registro de las alteraciones que han sufrido los yacimientos se ha incorporado ahora al conjunto de temas del modelo (Figura 6.4) y desde 1990 se ha progresado en el modo de describir con mayor detalle las condiciones de los sitios. . En este sentido, se han construido un conjunto importante de formatos con una intención gráfica (cartographic system of recording), con información sobre otras condiciones relativas al conjunto de alteraciones (Bednarik, 2001) del panel de la roca, tales como: áreas de exfoliación, presencia de líquenes, marcas de deterioros, intemperie de la roca, patina, minerales, sales). (*Include also information on other features of the rock panel, such as areas of exfoliation, lichen presence, taphonomic rock markings, patination, mineral accretions and salt efflorescence*-Bednarik, 2001). El objetivo es poder determinar simultáneamente la estructura total de los murales, las condiciones de los grupos, las características del conjunto de trazos y simultáneamente generar una evaluación gráfica, que permita ubicar en las paredes del yacimiento la ubicación exacta, de las perdidas del pigmento, la concentración de eventos fisicoquímicos que deterioran las pinturas o grabados, determinando 3n cada caso especifico, discriminado en parámetros (x, y) las condiciones de alteración y agentes de deterioro en porcentajes que le permiten evaluar estadísticamente el estado de un sitio y con ello las circunstancias que deberá conocer perfectamente quien quiera ser en el futuro administrador de los sitios.

En los últimos años el equipo de trabajo ha venido organizando trabajos adicionales sobre la ubicación de las zonas rupestres en los sistemas de información geográfica SIG y al terminar el trabajo de investigación de El Colegio Cundinamarca preparo un conjunto de mapas que permitían observar con mayor precisión la presencia de mas de 2000 rocas con grabados y con este procedimiento detenerse en el estudio de la densidades y comportamiento espacial de los sitios rupestres en una zona determinada (Figura 6.5). El conjunto complejo de capas, que se ubican en esta plataforma (Arcview) permite al investigador tener una imagen más precisa del comportamiento espacial de los yacimientos rupestres, sus condiciones en el área, las relaciones con la geomorfología de la zona y los posibles vínculos con otras zonas que igualmente contienen rocas. Esta herramienta de trabajo no solo permite evaluar los sitios y pensar relaciones, sino que se convierte en una nueva posibilidad para desarrollar nuevas preguntas sobre las concentraciones de las zonas rupestres en áreas específicas dentro del territorio y con estos sistemas de descripción es posible asociar otros yacimientos precolombinos (talleres de herramientas) y densidades que sin duda, permiten ampliar en conocimiento y explicación del entorno en el cual vivían las comunidades que realizaron los motivos rupestres.

Desde 1980 el equipo ha venido incorporando diversos temas al entorno de los computadores y en esta dinámica ha venido mirando con atención los programas que podrían ser más eficientes para producir desarrollos descriptivos. En lo relativo al avance de los registros de los murales es importante resaltar el manejo complejo que ahora se da a los mismos en el ámbito de la manipulación

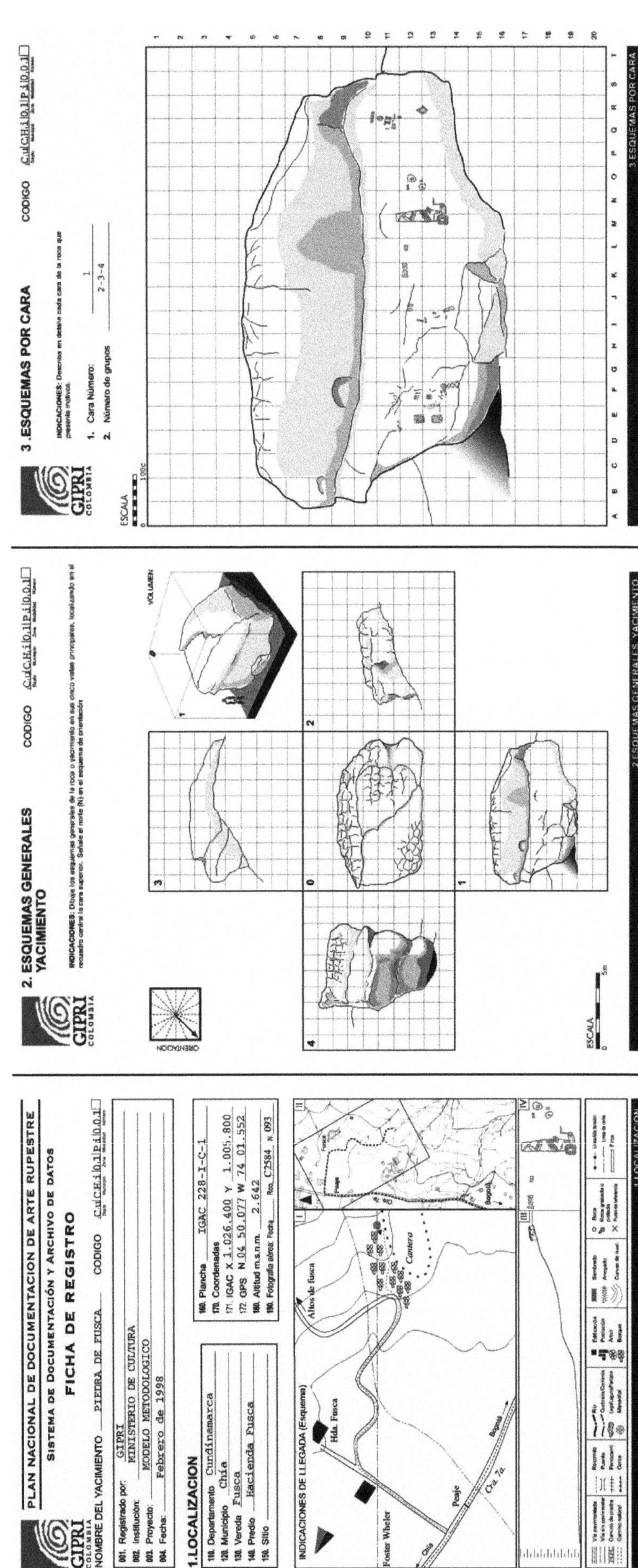

Fig. 6.2. Fichas de registro proyectos 1985-2000. En cada una de las etapas de investigación se fueron depurando los sistemas de registro. Aquí se muestran las fichas de localización, descripción general del yacimiento y descripción de los grupos de dibujos que aparecen sobre la pared de una roca, utilizando un sistema cartesiano. Roca de Fusca, Chía, 1997

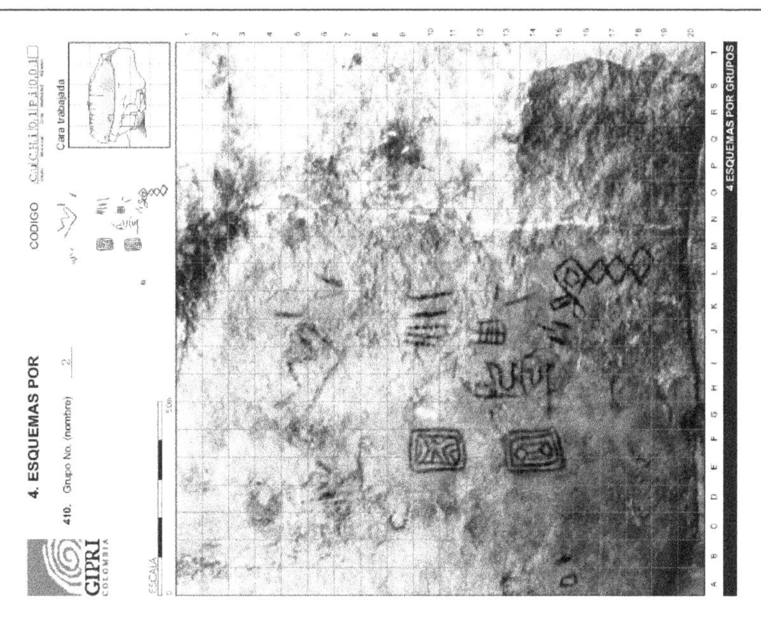

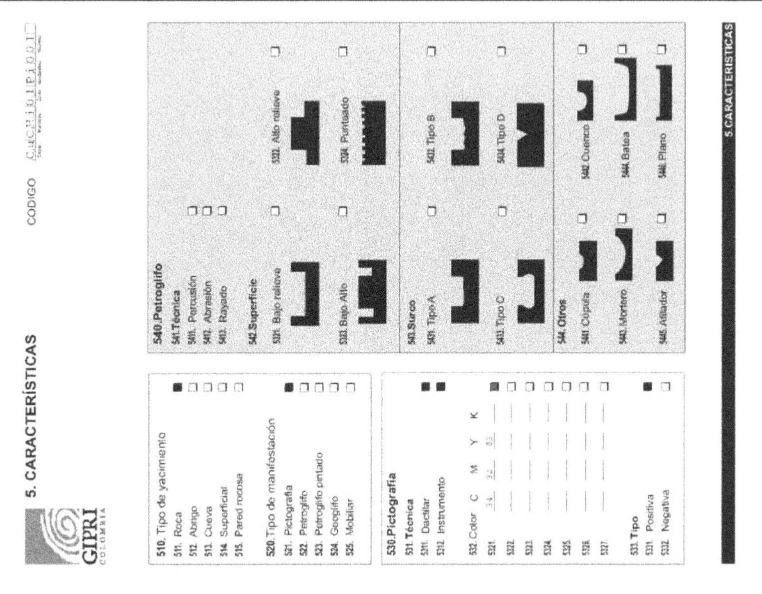

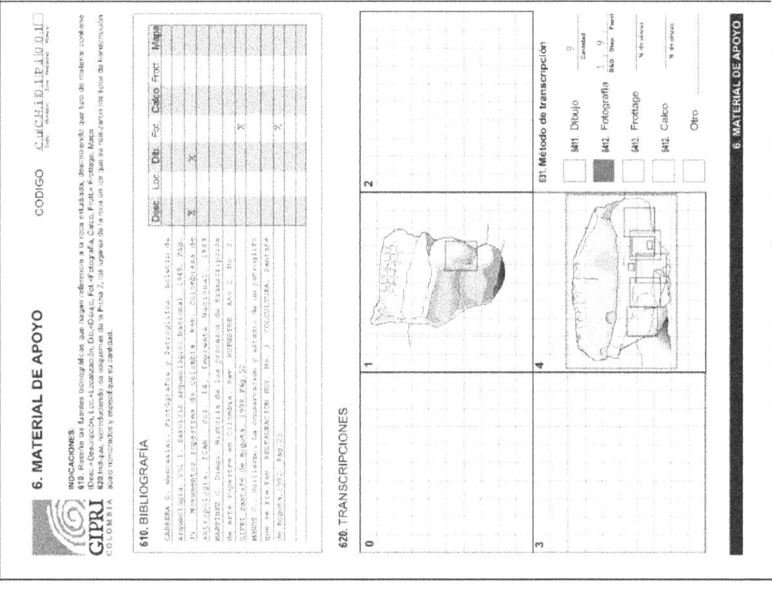

Fig. 6.3. *Fichas de registro proyectos 1985-2000.* En estas fichas se muestran los grupos pictóricos con alto grado de resolución, para ello es importante un buen registro fotográfico. También se describen las clases de arte rupestre registrado (pintura o petroglifo) y técnicas utilizadas para su ejecución. Roca de Fusca, Chía, 1997

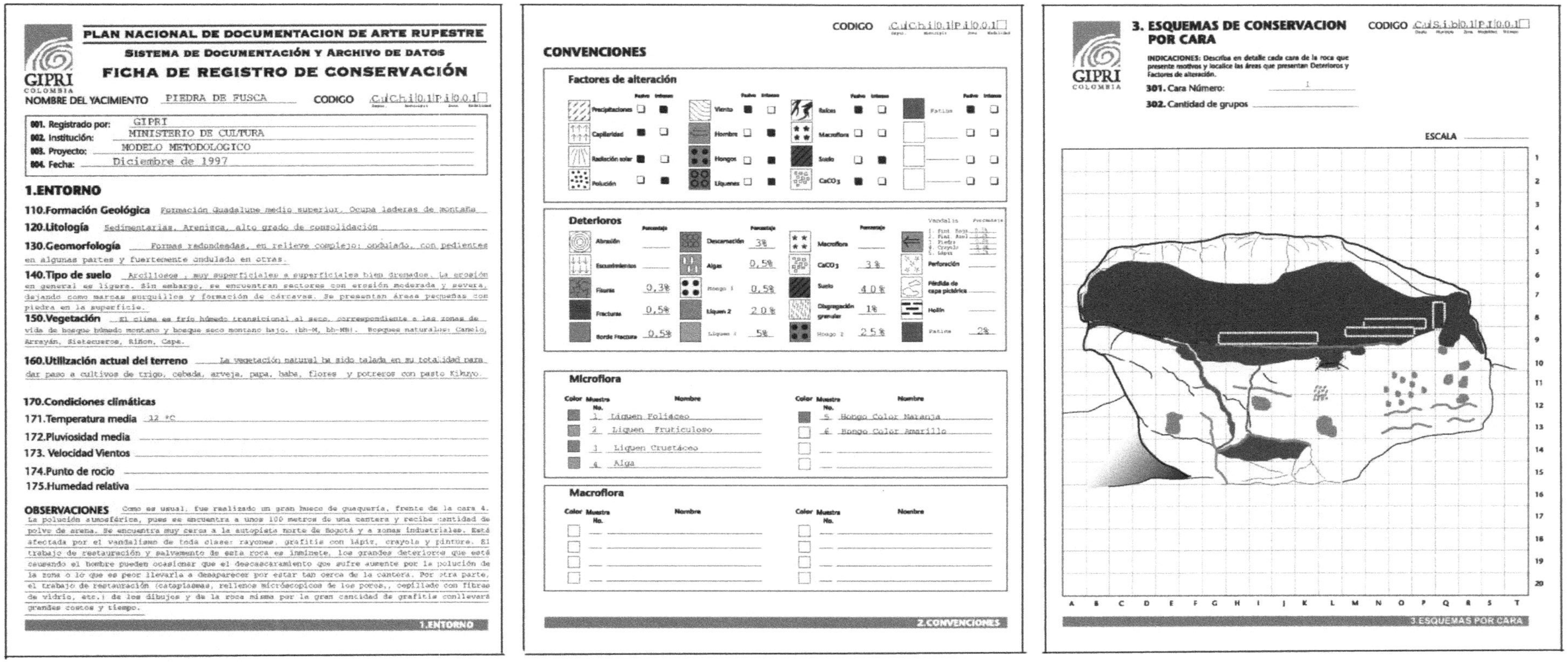

Fig. 6.4. *Fichas de registro proyectos 1985-2000.* Los trabajos de registro siempre van acompañados de las primeras evaluaciones sobre la conservación de los yacimientos rupestres. Para ello se han diseñado convenciones de colores que ayudan a identificar visualmente los deterioros y alteraciones que existen tanto en el sustrato como en los dibujos. Roca de Fusca, Chía, 1997

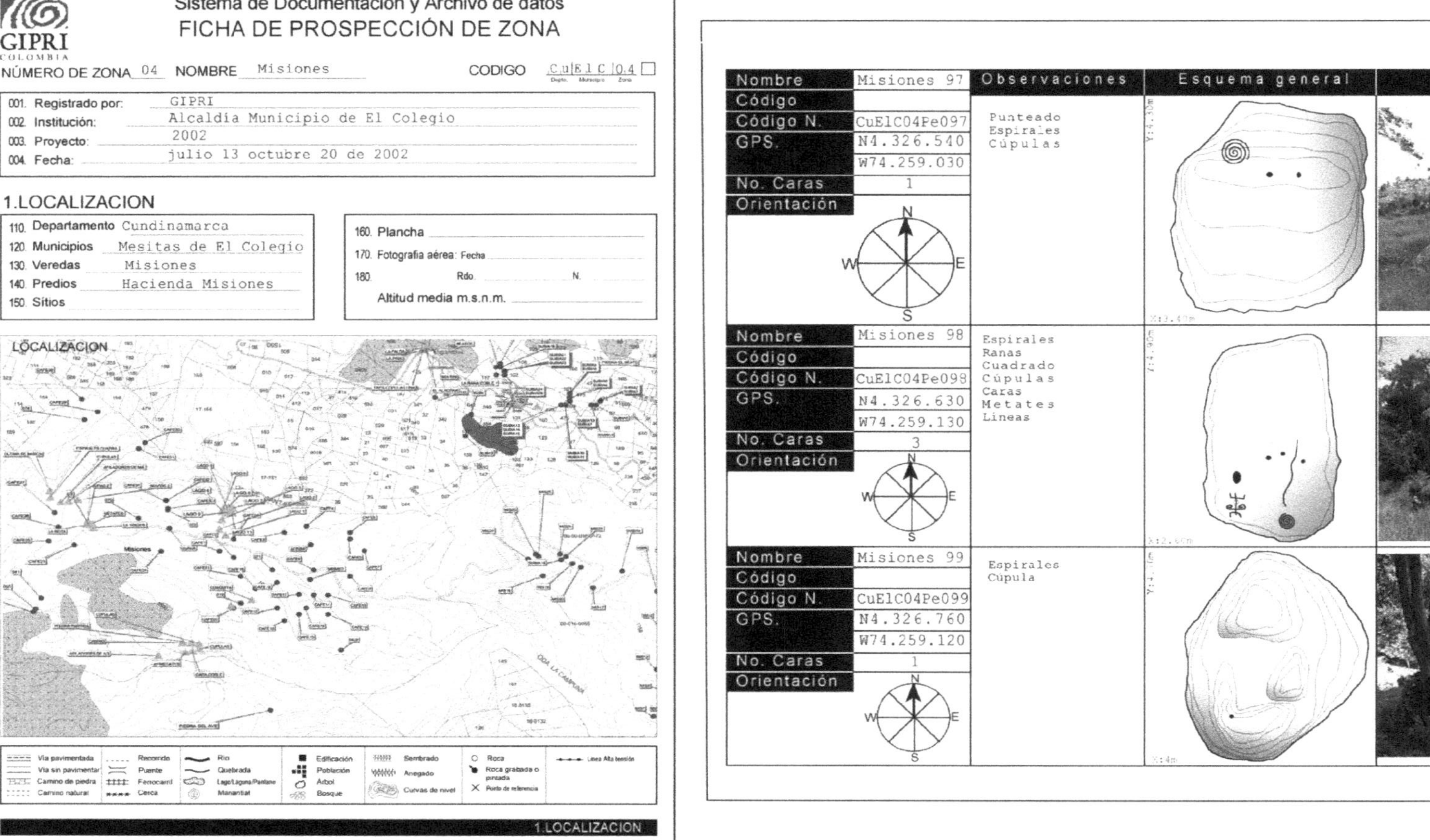

GIPRI COLOMBIA

PLAN NACIONAL DE DOCUMENTACION DE ARTE RUPESTRE

Sistema de Documentación y Archivo de datos

FICHA DE PROSPECCIÓN DE ZONA

NÚMERO DE ZONA 04 NOMBRE Misiones CODIGO CuE1C04

001. Registrado por: GIPRI
002. Institución: Alcaldía Municipio de El Colegio
003. Proyecto: 2002
004. Fecha: julio 13 octubre 20 de 2002

1.LOCALIZACION

110. Departamento Cundinamarca
120. Municipios Mesitas de El Colegio
130. Veredas Misiones
140. Predios Hacienda Misiones
150. Sitios

160. Plancha
170. Fotografía aérea: Fecha
180. Rdo. N.
Altitud media m.s.n.m.

LOCALIZACION

1.LOCALIZACION

CODIGO CuE1C04

Nombre	Misiones 97	Observaciones	Esquema general	Fotografía
Código		Punteado Espirales Cúpulas		
Código N.	CuE1C04Pe097			
GPS.	N4.326.540 W74.259.030			
No. Caras	1			
Orientación				
Nombre	Misiones 98	Espirales Ranas Cuadrado Cúpulas Caras Metates Lineas		
Código				
Código N.	CuE1C04Pe098			
GPS.	N4.326.630 W74.259.130			
No. Caras	3			
Orientación				
Nombre	Misiones 99	Espirales Cupula		
Código				
Código N.	CuE1C04Pe099			
GPS.	N4.326.760 W74.259.120			
No. Caras	1			
Orientación				

Fig. 6.5. Fichas de zona y SIG proyectos 2000-2004. En los últimos años las actividades de registro de zonas de arte rupestre han aumentado notablemente, por ello se ha hecho necesario sistematizar esta información y relacionarla con otros temas de investigación. Para ello se ha recurrido a los sistemas de información geográfica. Proyecto de registro y documentación del municipio de Mesitas de El Colegio, 1996-2004

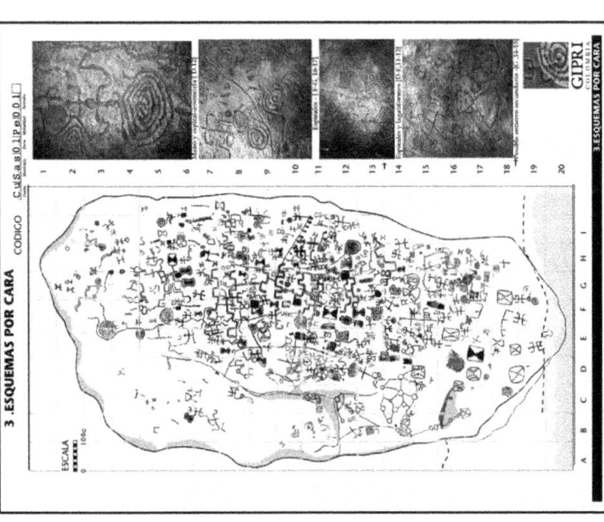

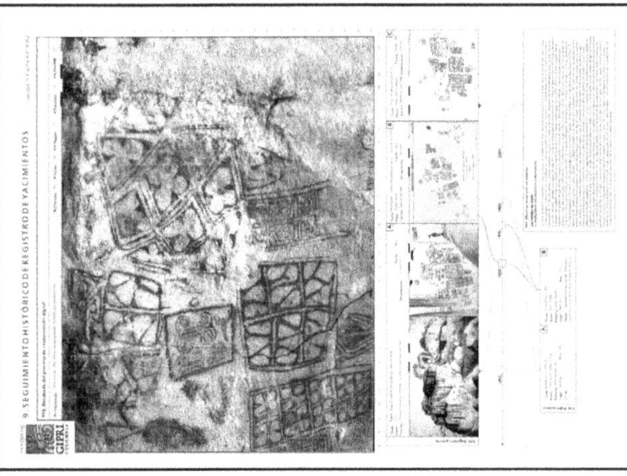

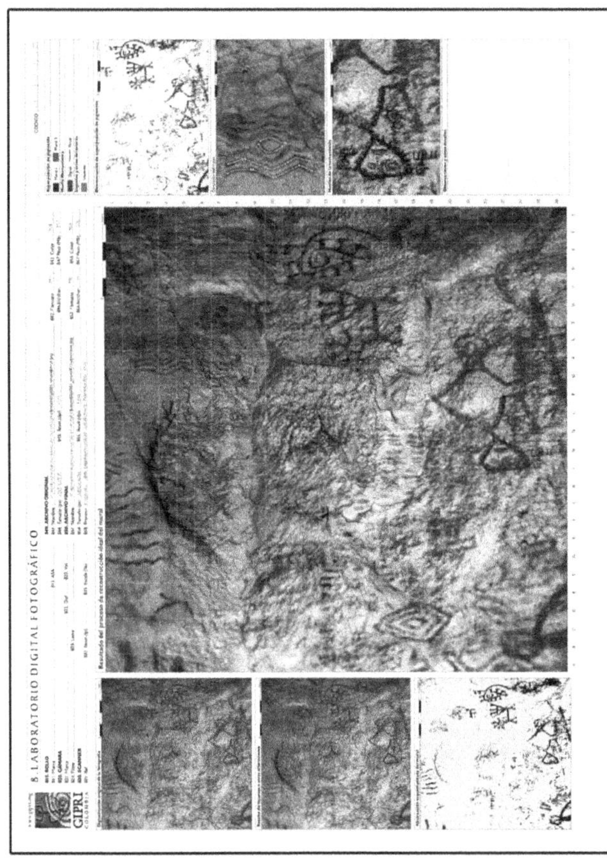

Fig. 6.6. *Reconstrucciones digitales 2004-2006.* Fotografía Guillermo Muñoz C.-Gipri. A- Documentación de petroglifos. Sasaima, Cundinamarca, 1998, (reformulación de la ficha, 2002). B- Seguimiento histórico de las transcripciones realizadas a un yacimiento. Pandi, Cundinamarca, 2004. C- Laboratorio Digital fotográfico y manipulación de imágenes. Ramiriquí, Boyacá, 2005

digital (Photoshop, Corel Draw, Phototrace). Ensamblar fotogramas de alta resolución y grano fino, generar procesos para visualizar aún mejor sus características, ubicar sus estructuras en cuadriculas cartesianas, determinar su alteración y singularidades (Figura 6.6) es ahora uno de los procesos de trabajo que realiza Gipri, con el propósito de describir y generar una documentación gráfica y geográfica de las zonas de estudio (Icomos, 2006).

Es necesario resaltar finalmente que los documentos producidos en los años setenta ingresaron sin dificultad alguna en las estructuras de las actuales tecnologías, que trabajan con sistemas de visualización semejantes.

Las zonas trabajadas por GIPRI tienen en resumen los siguientes materiales:

- Cartografía del lugar-(eventualmente aerofotografía de sector)
- Fotografía y material digital de los yacimientos en diferentes épocas (historia del registro)
- Fichas de zona y fichas de roca (discriminando los grupos pictóricos)
- Dibujos del yacimiento
- Historia de la investigación (diversas versiones)
- Digitalización de los materiales
- Bases de datos de los municipios y sitios rupestres
- Archivo fotográfico 70.000 fotos.

References

ANCIZAR, Manuel. (1850) *La peregrinación de Alfa.* Presidencia de la República. Bogotá.

CABRERA ORTIZ, Wenceslao. (1972) *Monumentos Rupestres de Colombia.* Cuaderno Primero: Generalidades. *Algunos Conjuntos Pictóricos de Cundinamarca.* Bogotá, Revista Colombiana de Antropología. Imprenta Nacional. Vol. 14.

CABRERA ORTIZ, Wenceslao. (1946) *Pictógrafos y Petroglifos.* Tomo II. Boletín de Arqueología. Bogotá.

BEDNARIK, Robert. (2001) *Rock art science: the scientific study of palaeoart* IFRAO-Brepols Volume 1, December.

GIPRI, Grupo de Investigación de la Pintura Rupestre Indígena:

GONZÁLEZ, Yaneth. (2000). *Zona del Tequendama. Transición entre pictografías y petroglifos. Avances de la investigación.* Revista Rupestre, Arte Rupestre en Colombia, No. 3, julio.

MARRINER, Harry. *Rock Artistas and skywatchers in ancient Colombia.* (1998). Bogotá, septiembre.

MARRINER, Harry. (1998). *Petroglifos: Una Breve Comparación De Tres Sitios.* Revista Rupestre, Arte Rupestre en Colombia, Año 2, No 2, agosto.

MARRINER, Harry. (2000). *Sitios con arte rupestre en el Valle de Subachoque.* Revista Rupestre, Arte Rupestre en Colombia, No. 3, julio.

MUÑOZ, Guillermo. (1980). *Rescatan 1.000 Dibujos Chibchas.* Rev. Cromos.

MUÑOZ, Guillermo. (1985). *Historia de la Investigación del Arte Rupestre en Colombia* (Altiplano Cundíboyacense 1a. versión), Congreso de Americanistas, Bogotá.

MUÑOZ, Guillermo. (1985). *GIPRI y la Investigación del Arte Rupestre* (Propuesta Metodológica), Congreso de Americanistas, Bogotá.

MUÑOZ, Guillermo. (1988). *El Petroglifo en el Altiplano Cundíboyacense* 46 Congreso Internacional de Americanistas, Holanda Amsterdam.

MUÑOZ, Guillermo. (1990). *Estado Actual de las Investigaciones en el Altiplano Cundíboyacense.* Simposio Administración del Patrimonio Arqueológico, Tema V. WAC 2, Venezuela.

MUÑOZ, Guillermo. (1991). *Estructura Cultural de Conservación del Arte Rupestre en el Altiplano Cundíboyacense.* Tercer Simposio Internacional de Arte Rupestre. Santa Cruz de la Sierra Bolivia.

MUÑOZ, Guillermo. (1998). *La Piedra de la Risa, la fiesta y las ofrendas.* Rupestre, Arte Rupestre en Colombia, No. 2, agosto.

MUÑOZ, Guillermo. (2000). *Covadonga: Primera Expedición Colombo-Francesa.* Revista Rupestre, Arte Rupestre en Colombia, No. 3, julio.

MUÑOZ, Guillermo. (2006) ICOMOS-CAR *Rock art of Latin America and the Caribbean* (http://www. icomos.org/studies/rockart-latinamerica/annex2.pdf).

RODRIGUEZ, Carlos. (1998). *Los Petroglifos Del Municipio Del Colegio: Modelo Sistemático De Registro.* Rupestre, Arte Rupestre en Colombia, No. 2, agosto.

TRUJILLO, Judith. (1998). *Aportes De La Tradición Oral En El Estudio Del Arte Rupestre Del Altiplano Cundiboyacense Colombianos.* Rupestre, Arte Rupestre en Colombia, No. 2, agosto.

ISAACS, Jorge. (1967). *Las Tribus Indígenas del Magdalena.* Sol y Luna, Bogotá.

TRIANA, Miguel. (1922) .*La Civilización Chibcha.* Escuela Tipográfica. Primera edición, Bogotá.

TRIANA, Miguel. *EL Jeroglífico Chibcha.*, Banco. Popular Bogotá, 1970.

TRIANA, Miguel. *Arte rupestre en Colombia.* Exposición itinerante, Banco de la República, Seccional Pereira. 1992.

NEW TECHNOLOGY FOR ROCK ART DOCUMENTATION BY THE SOPRINTENDENZA FOR ARCHAEOLOGICAL HERITAGE OF LOMBARDIA: LASER SCANNER IN VALLE CAMONICA (ITALY)

Emilio COLOMBO ZEFINETTI, Piergiorgio PEVERELLI

Via G. D'Alzano, 10, 24122 Bergamo, ITALY, E-mail: peverelli.colombo@tiscali.it

***Abstract**: Laser scanner technology applied to cultural heritage allows to obtain, in quick time, detailed monuments' plans useful to elaborate 3D models. For rock art this is really important because it allows to know the rock morphology and the rock surface conservation state. The paper shows the preliminary results about the use of laser scanner on a rock placed in Bedolina (Capo di Ponte, Brescia, Italy). The work was realized on 2005 by the Superintendence for Archaeological Heritage of Lombardy, that has the responsibility for preservation and conservation. It was structured in four steps: 1) topographic plan to define the targets; 2) series of photographs to obtain the final representation (scale 1:20); 3) representation in orthophoto; 4) 3D model elaboration.*

***Keywords**: Rock art, laser scanner, topographic plan, orthophoto, 3D model*

***Résumé**: L'utilisation du scanner laser permet d'obtenir, en peu de temps, des plans détaillés des monuments afin de reconstituer des models en 3D. Ceci est très important pour les gravures rupestres puisqu'il permet de connaître la morphologie de la roche et l'état de conservation de sa surface en même temps. L'article présent les résultats préliminaires sur l'utilisation du scanner laser sur une roche qui se trouve à Bedolina (Capo di Ponte, Brescia, Italie). Ce travail a été réalise in 2005 par la Surintendance pour l'héritage archéologique de la Lombardie qui est chargé de la préservation et de la conservation. On y retrouve 4 parties: 1) a plan topographique pour délimiter les objectives; 2) une série de photos pour obtenir la représentation finale (échelle 1:20); 3) une représentation en orthophoto et 4) l'élaboration du model en 3D.*

***Mots cles**: Gravures rupestres, scanner laser, plan topographique, orthophoto, model en 3D*

INTRODUCTION

The task of the mapping has always been the simplifycation of the reality in order to pick and to give back, with the best possible precision, a tightened selection of the geometrical characteristics of the analyzed object.

The traditional geometric mapping considers as critical elements of an entity the discontinuity points (the edge that characterizes the surfaces) recording the geometrical position on a projection plan, practically describing its contour. The new technologies of laser scanner mapping put aside from this selective choice, also because the object is not represented any more as a projection on the plan or 3D predetermined sights (axonometries, perspectives), but through a modifiable 3D model, constituted by a great number of points. For all these points it is possible to know relations, position and colours; they do not define intersections of plans but, with good approximation, entire surfaces.

COMPARISON BETWEEN LASER SCANNER AND PHOTOGRAMMETRY

We have used photogrammetry since 1995 and so we can make a useful comparison between the two methodologies similar in the phase of data acquisition but different for accuracy.

Photographic relief

In the photogrammetry differently from the mapping with laser scan, you have to double the quantity of the photos. It uses the principle of superimposition of the images in order to recreate the three-dimensionally in the restitution phase. The photos must be as possibly parallels to the medium plan of the investigated object. It is difficult to realize the mobile structures useful to capture the images. With the laser scan technology one can also execute angle shots in the limit of a correct description of the morphology of the surveyed object.

Topographical relief

Referring to the previous voice it can be deduced that the points of support to the photographic mapping are approximately 50% more in the photogrammetric one. All this involves a meaningful increase of the time for positioning sights and making topographical struck.

Determination of the D.T.M

The procedure to determinate the D.T.M in the two methodologies is different: with laser scanning the creation of D.T.M takes place in loco while with photogrammetry it is made in office during the restitution phase. We must therefore specify that in photogrammetry is the man who characterizes the precision of D.T.M determination, through the correct collimation of the points of the surface. The time to elaborate a model with the same number of points is remarkably inferior with the laser scan method (determination of 1800 points to the second against approximately 1-2 points at a second).

Ortophoto and 3D model

For this phase there are not particular differences between the two technologies, the difference is deriving from previously described operations. In fact the models described by the laser scan, by number of acquired points, have a lot of information and the geometric description of the object to investigate is more precise.

Conclusions

Referring to the morphology of the ground and the geometries of the surveyed object, we think more correct to use the laser scan technology above all in archaeology, where the step of the 1,5 scansions can reach up to millimeter (1 cm in the architectonic sector). These scansion steps generate the D.T.M., which reaches easily several million points. The result is seldom reached in photogrammetry and with a very high costs (it is enough to analyze the time of data acquisition of the two methodologies and transform them in hours man).

LASER SCANNING APPLIED TO ROCK ART

On 2005, in accordance with the Superintendence for Archaeological Heritage of Lombardy, the laser scanner technology was used on a new rock found in Bedolina (Capo di Ponte, Brescia, Italy). The rock was engraved during prehistory with topographic maps, a type of figures very common in this area of the Valle Camonica.

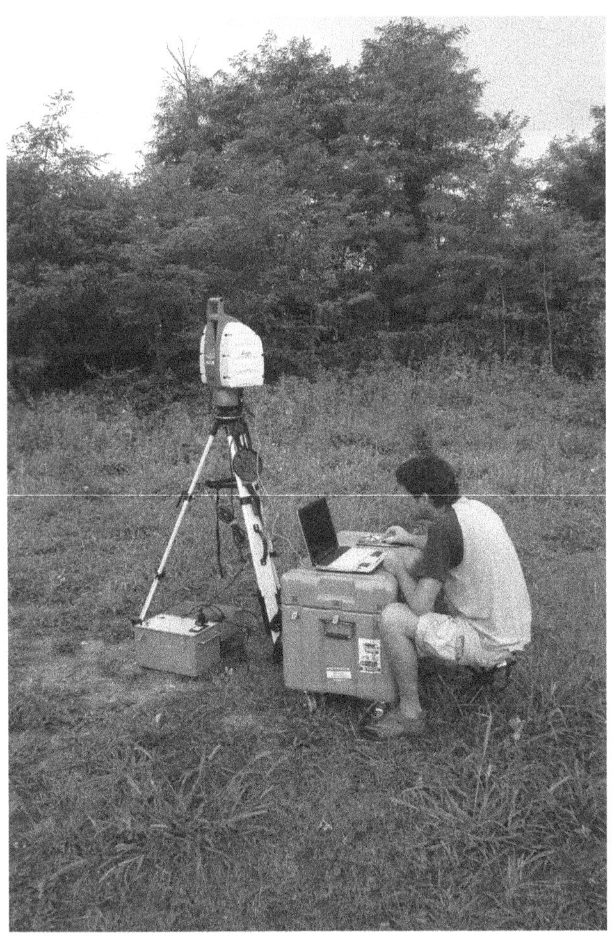

Fig. 7.1. Laser scanner Leica HDS 3000, connected to a notebook

This paper presents the main steps of the laser-scanning processing chain, from the acquisition of the object to the three-dimensional model.

The work was structured in:

- topographical mapping for the determination of support points for a correct union of the several laser scansions in the space;
- photographic shots taken for the restitution in scale 1/20;
- orthophoto graphical restitution;
- creation of a 3D model.

The execution of the described mapping involves methodological steps divided in operations in open field (photographic, topographical relief and laser scansions) and operations in office.

PHOTOGRAPHIC MAPPING

After a careful inspection, where we analysed the physical characteristics of the rock and the scale of final restitution (1:20 scale), we decided to use the digital semimetric camera Nikon D100 with f. 20.58mm for all the photographic shots.

The procedure involves the execution of different operations:

- photographic mapping survey of the rock;
- photographic mapping survey of the rock and position of the topographical targets useful for the determination of the orthophoto.

The photos, where possible, have been taken parallel to the medium plan of the investigated surface by means of telescopic tripods.

TOPOGRAPHICAL MAPPING

The next operations are photographic shots and spatial acquisition of the trigonometric points. This kind of operation is necessary for the determination of a general net of the object, due to the acquaintance, in the space of support points, for the photographic survey (target acquisition) and for the determination of support points in order to unify different laser scansions (target acquisition).

For the procedure of the topographical survey we used the total motorized Leica 1201 TCRA 300 station with angular precision of 1". This station has incorporated a coaxial diastimeter to the tracking telescope, which uses a method of measurement at laser impulses, ideal for the determination of the distance without using the reflector

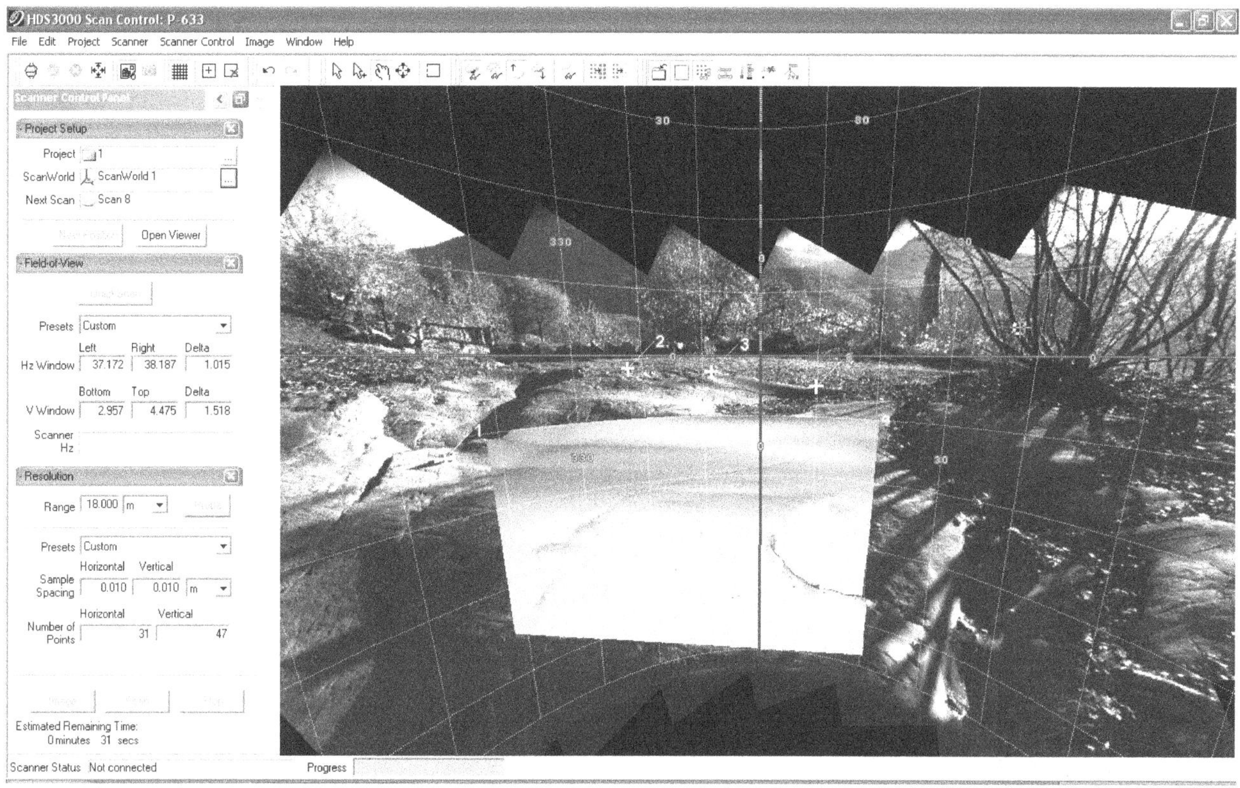

Fig. 7.2. Superimposition of the points on the photo

up to a capacity of approximately 500 m with a doubt of 3mm+3ppm.

The capacity depends naturally on the brightness of the atmosphere and on the reflection of the target. The intensity of the reflected line depends on the structure of the surface, on the material that it is made of and on the angle between the hit face and the beam. For these reasons is necessary to have points on the ground from which it is possible to have a correct frame of the sections to determine.

THREE-DIMENSIONAL LASER SCANNER PROGRAM

The system laser scanner HDS 3000 of Leica Geosystems is employed for the execution of the three-dimensional scansions. This instrument, measuring the time of distance of the laser impulses, is able to determine a space cloud of 1800 points at a second with a precision of ± 2mm on range 1m-50m. With this new relief methodology, the data acquisition phase is enormously reduced in consideration of the time employed to achieve results comparable with other sophisticated instruments (see photogrammetry); the geometric precision is remarkable, so as the thoroughness of the details.

The instrument is connected to a software data acquisition, which allows to select the step and the scan area.

The operation to select the scan area is facilitated by the possibility to execute spherical shots all around. There are then remarkable analogies between the way which the scanner acquires information and the human eye: both observe an object by a well known position. One deduces that in order to measure and control an object it is necessary to observe it from all the points of view useful to the thoroughness of the mapping. For this reason, the single scansions have to be connected with topographical measures.

The scanning area comes overlapped to the photographic image.

During the acquisition it is possible to see point-clouds in three-dimensional sights, where the single point reflects the reflectance of the material. In the case of the rock of Bedolina it has been used a mesh step of 2x2 millimeter.

It is just the defined regularity and uniformity of the grid, on which the information are assumed, to guarantee the systematicity and objectivity of the data. Such grid must be more or less thick (resolution or step of scansion) according to the characteristics of the investigated surfaces. This is one of the fundamental choices to make, with one's own experience, in the process of data acquisition. As far as the supposed amount of the data, the highest imaginable resolution always constitutes a sampling of the surveyed entities. Besides, the overdetermination is an essential parameter in the survey operations in order to allow evaluation on the achieved precision.

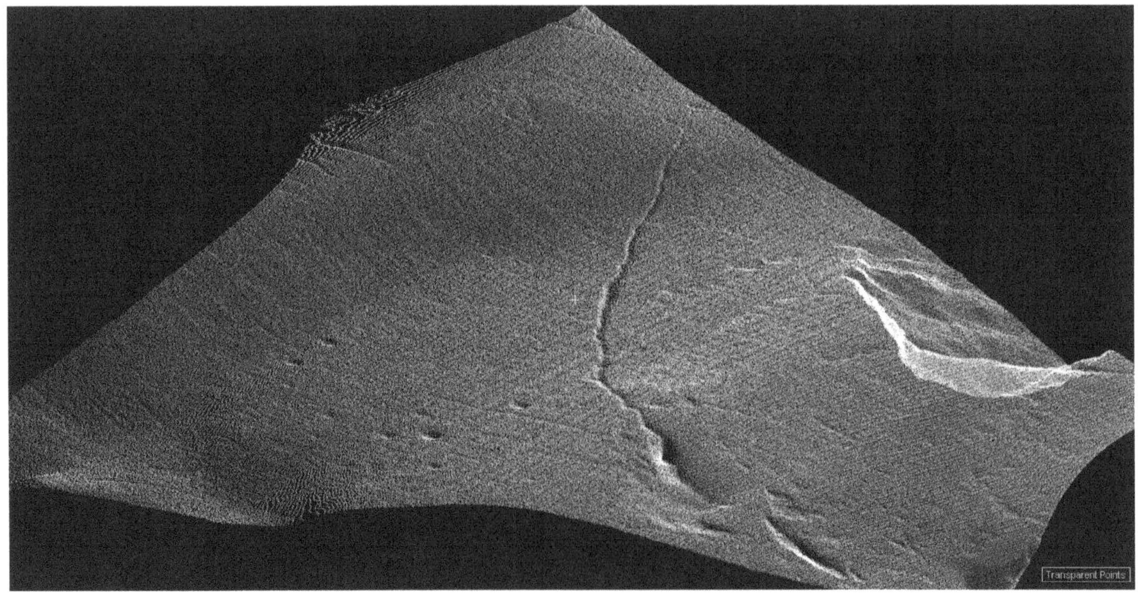

Fig. 7.3. 3D vision realized with 2x2 mm step scansion. The colour reflects the optical characteristic of the material

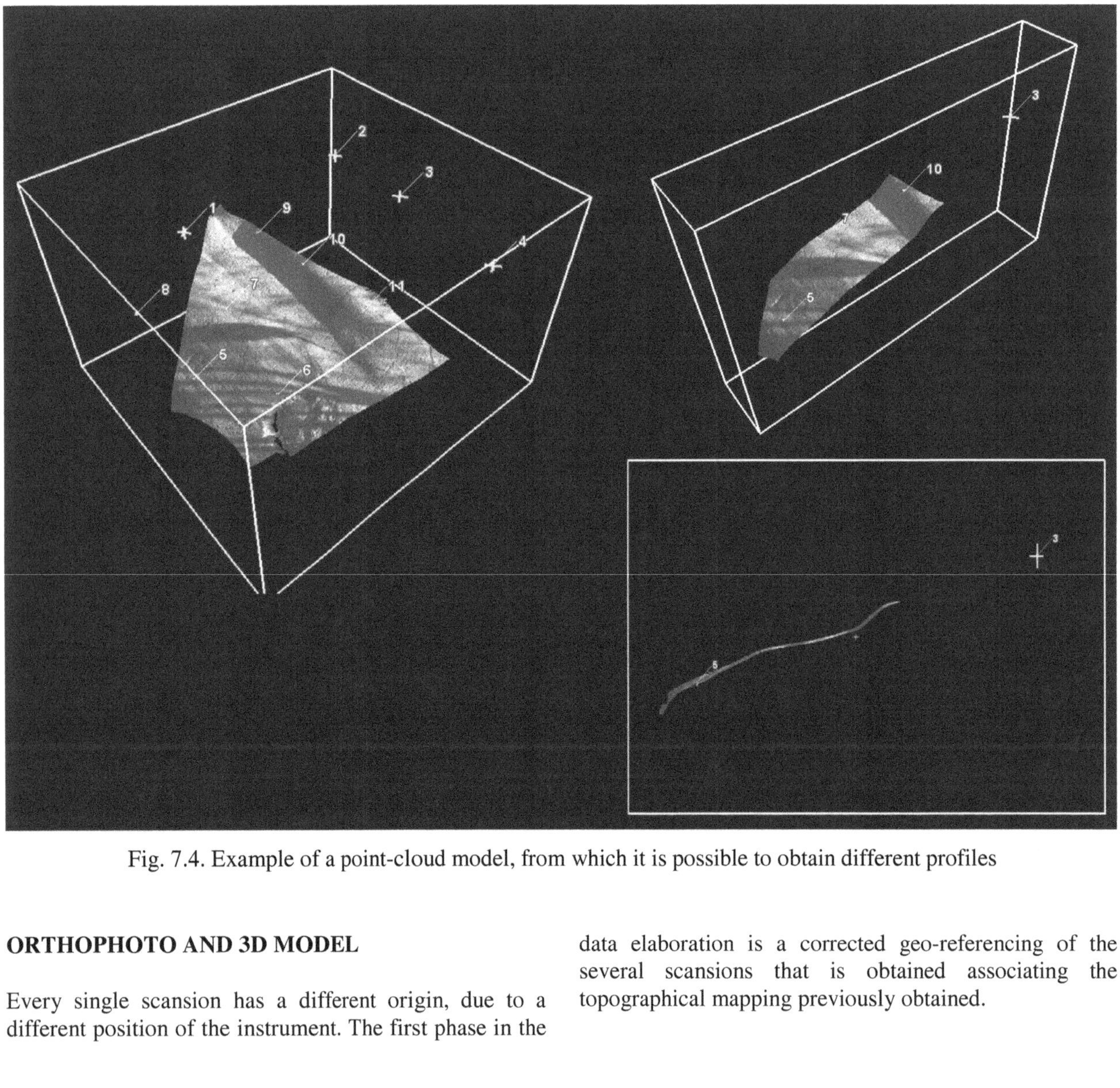

Fig. 7.4. Example of a point-cloud model, from which it is possible to obtain different profiles

ORTHOPHOTO AND 3D MODEL

Every single scansion has a different origin, due to a different position of the instrument. The first phase in the data elaboration is a corrected geo-referencing of the several scansions that is obtained associating the topographical mapping previously obtained.

From this obtained model, it is possible to execute different operations:

- colouration of the model which passes from one coloration of reflectance to RGB;
- determination of sights sections.

After the union of several point-clouds (generated from the laser scanning), it is necessary to create a triangulated model on which will be projected in succession several photos for the orthophoto and a three-dimensional model.

Now it is possible to associate digital images of the object, in order to achieve orthophotographs with photo-realistic effects, transforming the model of points into a model of surfaces.

The creation of the ortophotography is generated by the determination of the projection plan and the choice of the photos, by which it will be composed.

Another remarkable advantage is the possibility of managing the model with an application of Autocad which allows different operations such as

- vectorial drawing of the model;
- determination of profiles;
- projection plans can be executed.

DIGITAL RIGHTS MANAGEMENT FOR ARCHIVED PICTURES IN WEB CONTEXTS

Daniele VITALI, Luca MEGALE
E-mail: daniele@oldsail.net, E-mail: luca_megale@yahoo.it

Abstract: *Archives that offer a web-based access often publish images. Those images are used for different purposes (i.e. didactic, personal, etc.) and such availability requires to protect the cultural heritage in order to avoid commercial use of published images and to protect intellectual property. The paper describes an innovative method which uses advanced watermarking techniques in conjunction with a Digital Rights Management system based on strong digital signatures, in order to enable web archives to publish protected images and have a legal proof of ownership of them.*
Keywords: *Digital Rights Management, photographic heritage, internet*

Résumé: *Les archives, qui proposent un accès basé sur le web, publiant souvent des images. Ces images sont publiées pour des buts différents (p.e. didactique, personale, etc.) et une telle disponibilité exige la protection de l'héritage culturel de façon à éviter l'utilisation commerciale des images éditées et aussi à protéger la propriété intellectuelle. L'article présent une méthode innovatrice qui utilise des techniques avancées de marquage numérique avec un système de Gestion des Droits Numériques basés sur des signatures numériques fortes, de façon que les archives web puissent publier des images protégées en ayant une preuve légale de leur appartenance.*
Mots cles: *Gestion des Droits Numériques, héritage photographique, Internet*

INTRODUCTION

Until the spread of digital cameras archives used to contain printed pictures and films. Copies weren't exactly as the original, and quality degeneration was a sort of automatic protection of those images. Digital images introduced new concerns: copies are exactly the same image as the original. Two categories of problems are born: copyright protection and copy prevention. The first is a ownership and legal problem: how do I prove that an image is mine? I do not own anymore the only original picture and identical copies can be spread. Anybody can claim the ownership, and I can do very little to prevent it. The second is a technical problem: how do I prevent wild spread of valuable images, for example contained in my archive?

Nowadays most archives allow access through internet. A picture on the web is highly exposed to abuse: anybody that can see a picture can copy it. This context introduces problems that have not yet been fully resolved, and the restriction policies used for printed pictures archives are unsuited to solve them.

The first solution that the research community came up with was cryptography. Images were placed in an encrypted package before distribution and access was granted only to those who knew the password. This model was proved to be weak: beside technical solutions to open the package, it was excessively user dependant. After the package was opened the user still had a copy of the original image impossible to distinguish, and the problem was still in place.

A solution to both ownership problem and technical distribution is watermark. This paper introduces a broader definition of watermark, speaking of visible and invisible techniques. A watermark is an image modification that allows information insertion into it, both in a visible or invisible manner. As shown in Fig. 8.1, both techniques aren't mutually exclusive.

The technique use to insert hidden information within an image is called *steganography*, the art and science of writing hidden messages in such a way that no one apart from the intended recipient knows of the existence of the message. Invisible watermarks do not change the signal to a perceptually great extent, but provides a mechanism to track the picture to the original owner. Their existence is hided. Visible watermarks change the picture in way that watermarked pictures are visually different from the original, for example adding an image as a watermark to another image. Their existence is known. Stock photography agencies often add a watermark in the shape of a copyright symbol ("©") to previews of their images, so that the previews do not substitute for high-quality copies of the product included with a license.[1]

RELATED WORK

The market of image protection attracted over the years many players, both from industry and academy. Many companies sell software components to avoid image abuse in web contexts, both using invisible and visible watermarking techniques. Most of them apply to one image at the time and their effectiveness is often questionable. For example one of the most important software companies offering watermark services is

[1] Wikipedia, Steganography and Digital watermarking definition, http://en.wikipedia.org/, last accessed 2006-10-15.

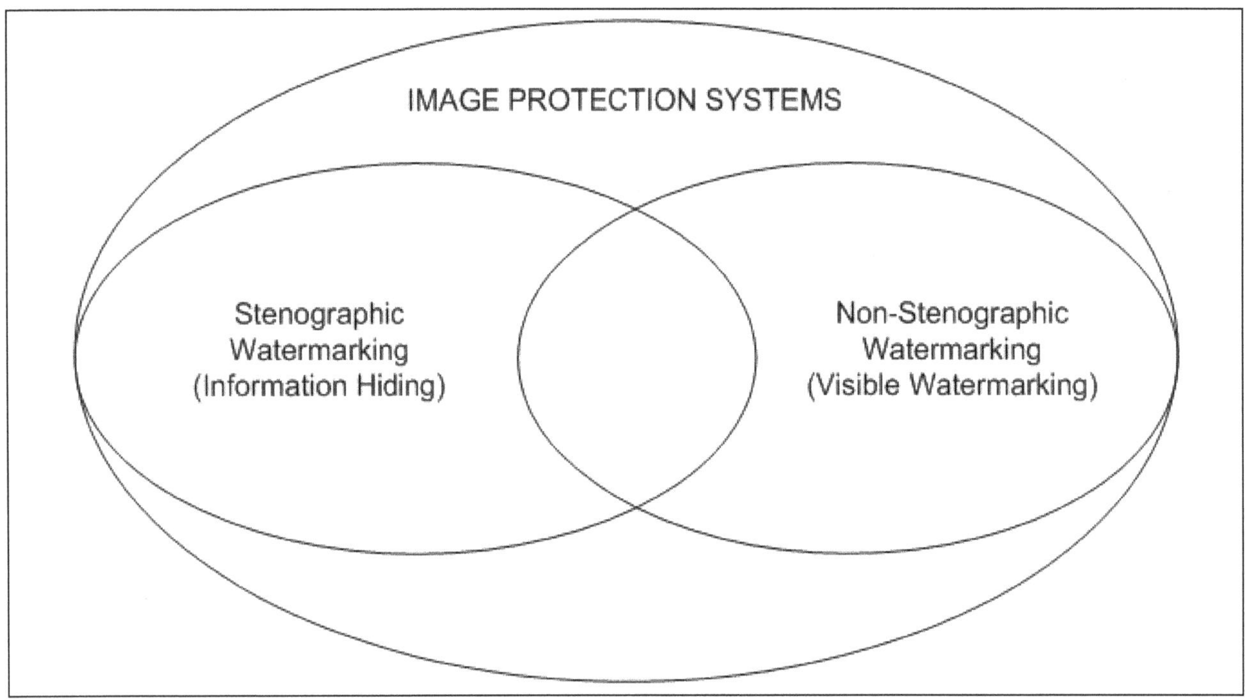

Fig. 8.1. Image Protection Domain

Digimarc®.[2] Their invisible watermark component is included in Adobe Photoshop® (look at the 'filters' section) and is one of the most effective.

We will do now guided test, in order to test the effectiveness of it:

Step 1) Load the original image in Adobe Photoshop® (Fig. 8.2).

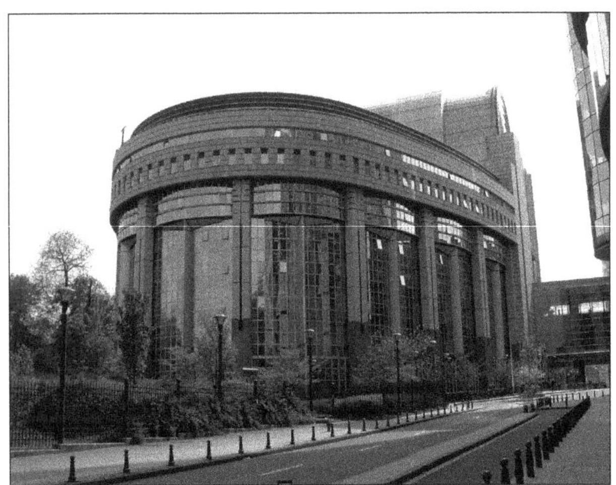

Fig. 8.2. Original image

Step 2) Embed a unique ID inside the image (Fig. 8.3), you will find it in the Filters section of Adobe Photoshop®.

[2] Digimarc. *Invisible Watermarking software*, http://www.digimarc.com/

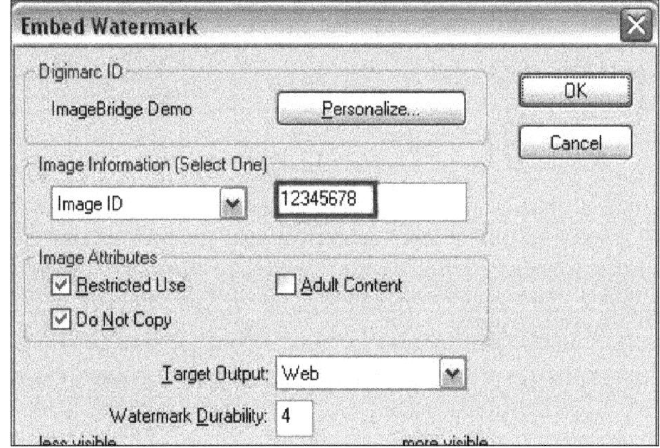

Fig. 8.3. Digimarc invisible watermark adding interface

The result is an image that is very similar to the original. Carefully looking at it you will see some quality degradation. That is because some parts of the image that before was carrying colour information are now carrying our ID. Some degree of degradation is inevitable.

Step 3) Modify the image, for example cropping the most important part (Fig. 8.4).

Step 4) Run the "Read Watermark" tool within Adobe Photoshop®, you will see the ID (Fig. 8.5).

The test can give positive or negative results, depending on the image modification. For large images, applying a strong modification will lead to a negative result.

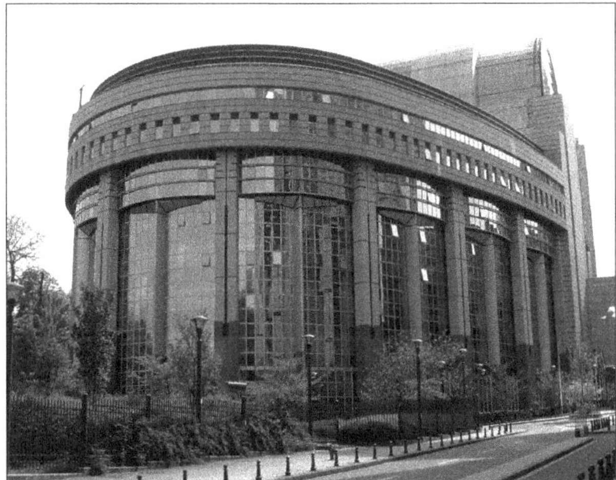

Fig. 8.4. Cropped image with embedded watermark

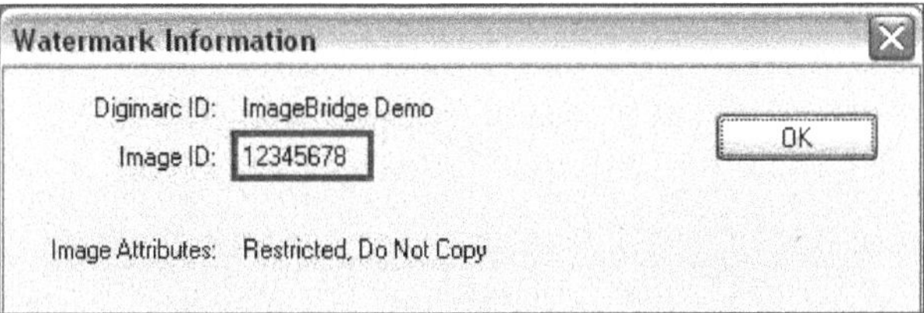

Fig. 8.5. Watermark recognition

We saw how to protect a single image using invisible watermark techniques but we are still far from an effective image protection archive integration. Large archives need to support the procedure we saw automatically, and supply more than one technique.

TECHNICAL PROTECTION

As seen in the related work section of this paper 100% technical protection cannot be achieved. Combining the shown techniques can improve security but and strong integration into web applications is needed. The techniques that we will cover are: visible watermark, steganography, automatic image resizing and we will briefly cover the legal protection matter. Large archives need full integration, since manual modification is a very time consuming task. Our approach is to consider the dispatching of images in web contexts as a service offered by the cataloguing system itself, in order to reduce time needed by operators. Figure 8.6 shows the service structure.

Within this deployment model the service modifies the source image at runtime, so that the high quality source is never exposed to the end user. Modifications are

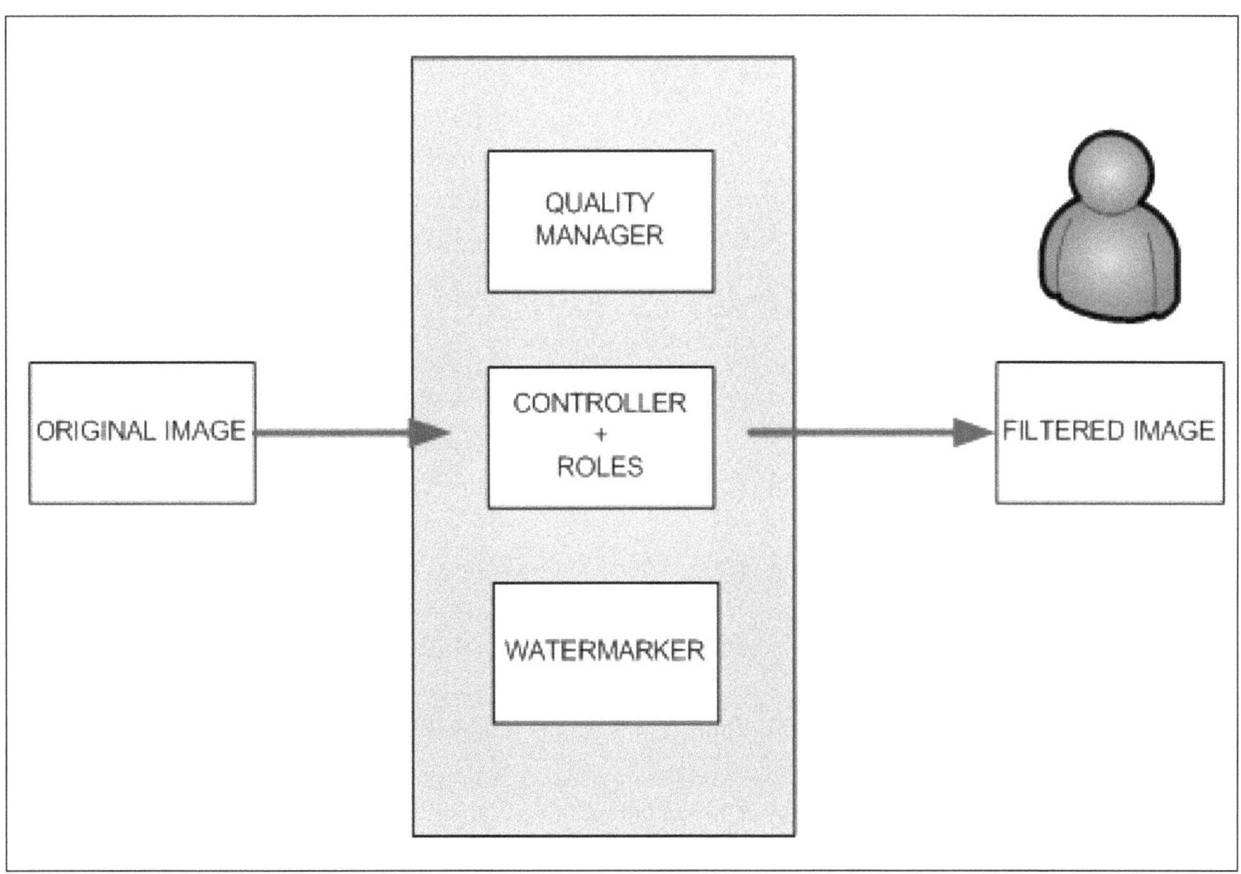

Fig. 8.6. Service architecture for image protection

dynamically applied to the image, depending on context parameters such as user profile or use (i.e. printing vs visualization on the PC monitor)

Moreover, abuse detection need to be integrated into the workflow in a way that technical and legal procedures are explicit both to the end user and the operator. Watermark techniques always provide mechanisms to track the image to the original owner.

Watermarking techniques

Digital watermarking is a technique which allows an individual to add hidden copyright notices or other verification messages to digital audio, video, or image signals and documents.

In literature those techniques are often classified in two main streams: *visible watermarking techniques* and *invisible watermarking techniques.*

Visible watermarking techniques

The original image is modified, often adding copyright information in the shape of the company logo or of the copyright symbol ("©"). The final image is different from the source and the added information is known to the end user. The output quality is often lowered by visible watermarks since the objective is to protect the most valuable parts of the source image. This technique is unpractical for some uses, such as the web publishing of rock art images in which the end user wants to enjoy every valuable part of it without interferences (Fig. 8.7).

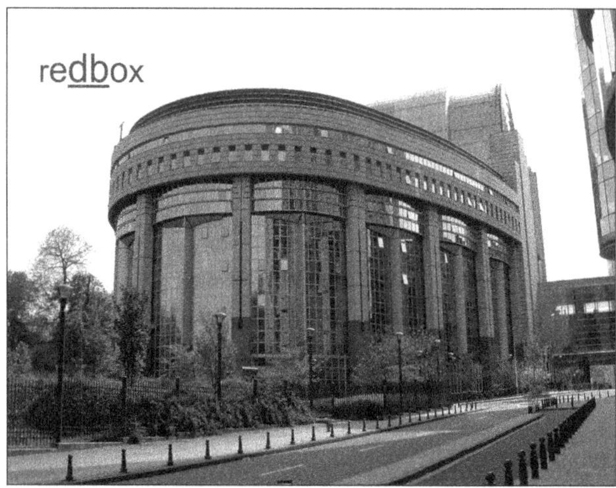

Fig. 8.7. Visible watermark addition

This technique is the most secure way to protect images because of the technical difficulty in removing the added mark.

The image shown in Fig. 8.8 describe the workflow in adding visible watermarks.

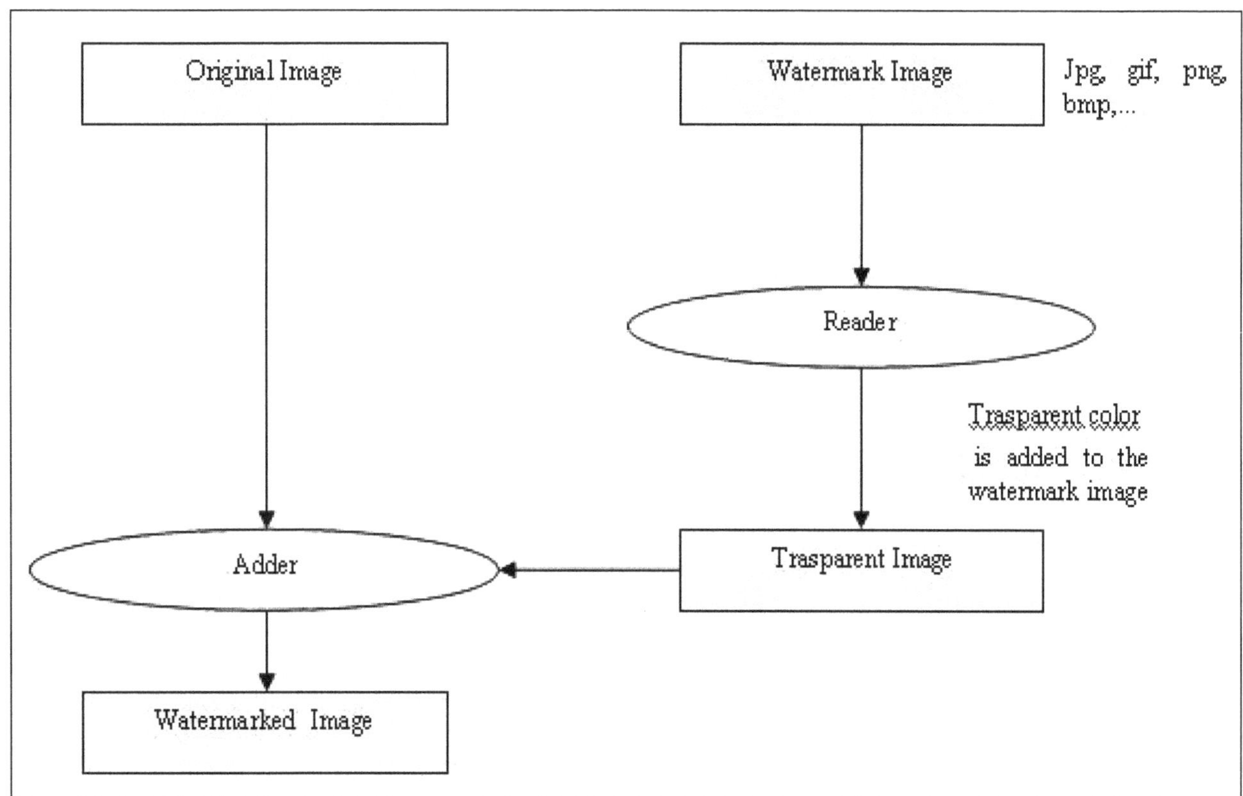

Fig. 8.8. Workflow in adding visible watermarks

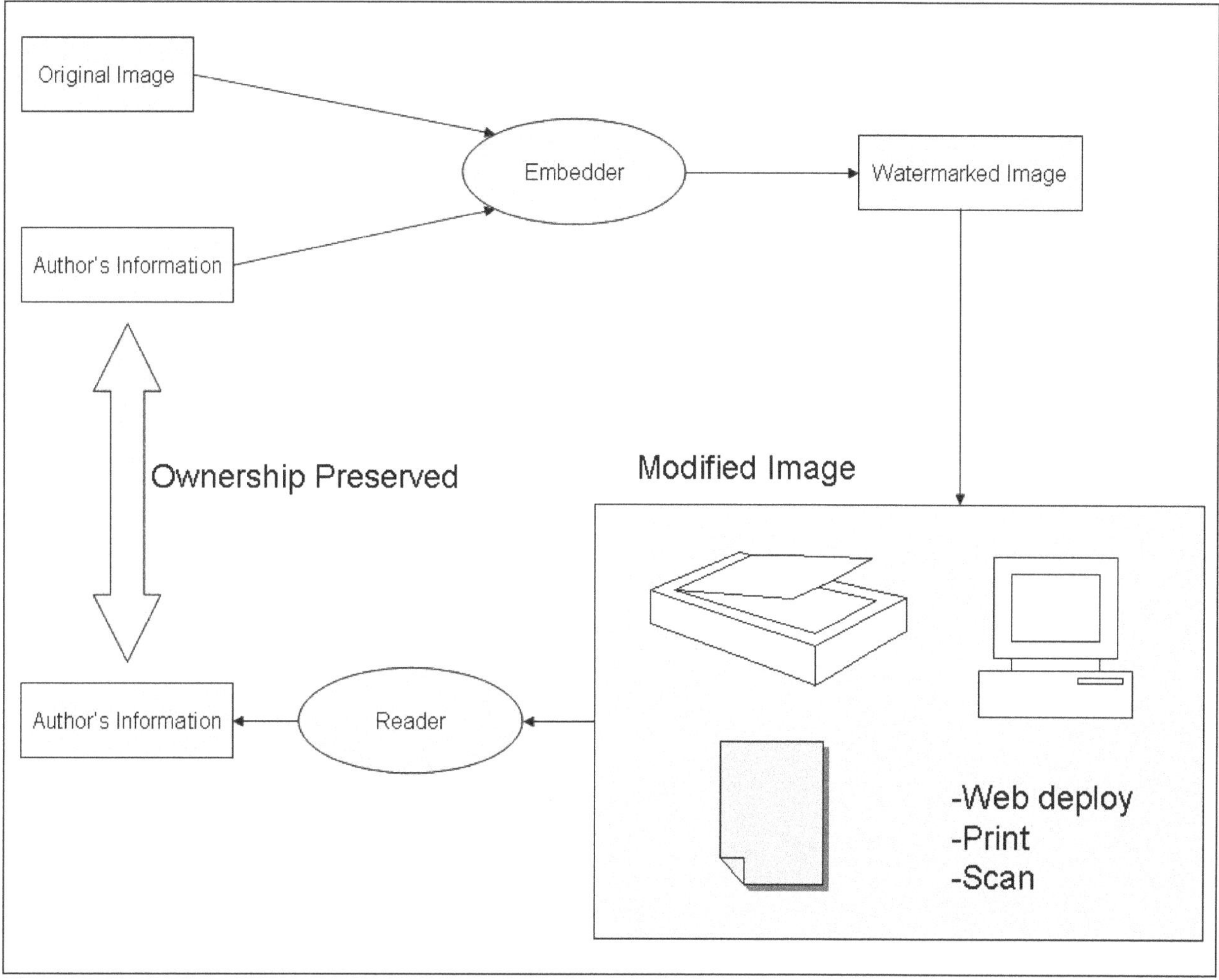

Fig. 8.9. Invisible watermark addition and recognition

Invisible watermarking techniques

Invisible watermarks do not change the image to a perceptually great extent, i.e., there are only minor variations in the output. Invisible watermarks that are unknown to the end user are called "steganographic".

The original image quality cannot be preserved, and this makes the technique non usable in some contexts (such as printing).

The diagram shown in Fig. 8.9 illustrates the workflow for adding and later detecting an invisible watermark.

How to remove a watermark

How strong are the shown techniques? The image protected with a visible watermark can be cropped. Removing an invisible watermark can be more difficult, since we do not always know what algorithm has been used and we cannot be sure of the removal. We know that this technique can resist some degree of cropping, image resizing, format conversion. We could easily prove that a combination of these three simple operations can prevent the reader component (Fig. 8.9) from recognizing the author information.

Image quality modification techniques

An image can be modified by different means. It can automatically be transformed with some degree of degradation. The parameters that can be altered are size, compression, color depth.

This paper introduces a good practice named "Minimum Needed Quality" (MNQ):

> *"The output of a image request should never be the original source but a modified version of it. Modification should be done on the base of user profile and use of the image. The output should be the in the lowest quality and size in order to be usable in the target context."*

Source image storage

The source image must be protected and never "exposed" to requester. Only particular accesses can be granted, and only to accredited people.

Modification based on user profile

An important statement from the MNQ good practice is that the user profile influences the output quality. For example, we could state that in our archive Administrators have access to the maximum quality images, and Guests have only access to low quality thumbnails.

Modifications based on usage

A second important statement is that final usage of the image influences the output. For example, images needed for web visualization are printed to screen with fixed width, while images requested for printing need to have a greater size.

More techniques or implementation examples:[3][4][5][6][7][8]

LEGAL PROTECTION

Copyright laws are in constant evolution. New technologies such as digital signatures are strongly influencing the community. Image abuse (such as using images for publications without the written permission from the owner) is a legal problem. In this paper we show a technique is named CopyZero[9] that has been ideated by the Italian *Costozero movement*. The mechanism relies on the legal value of digital signatures and timestamps. A digital signature is a technology that is spreading and its legal value is being recognized in almost all industrialized countries. It is based on private/public keys.[10] Keys are the basis of digital protection. If the key (sometimes called a password) is only known by authorized individual(s), the data cannot be exposed to other parties. Only those who know the key can decrypt it. This is known as 'private key' cryptography, which is the most well known form.[11]

CopyZero proves that a specific author generated an artwork, and that the artwork existed at a specific time.

How does it work?

Step 1) convert any artwork in a digital format. In the case of digital photography use the source image.

Step 2) prepare the license and copyright data in a digital format. Digitally sign and apply a legal timestamp (can be purchased from official web services)

Step 3) enclose the artwork and the signed files into a package. Digitally sign and apply a legal timestamp to the whole package

This technique would allow abuse detection to be legally effective. Many times detected abuses cannot be punished. The shown mechanism is useful for large archives, since a single timestamp and signature can be placed on an archive containing many different files.

DIGITAL RIGHTS MANAGEMENT ARCHITECTURE

An archive oriented architecture must sustain administrators and operators in the process of digital image protection. Figure 8.10 shows a detailed components schema of a system that is able to automatically protect multimedia contents.

Each user is assigned a role within the system on which the correct filters are selected. For example Administrators can have access to full quality images, while Guests can only have access to lowered quality images shipped with an embedded invisible watermark. There is no need to use only one DRM technique that can easily be executed in sequence. We showed that information addition within an image can result in sensibly lowered quality; the use of different techniques in sequence can produce too much 'noise' added to the source media.

Users are also added to a group. Groups are used to define the resources a user has access to. For example in medium sized archives multimedia contents are divided in categories and different users edit and view only some of them. The combination of user roles and groups enable a fully customizable authorization model.

---

[3] EIKONAmark. *Invisible Watermarking software,* http://www.alphatecltd.com/watermarking/eikonamark/eikonamark.html.

[4] *Invisible Watermark Tutorial,* http://www.deviantart.com/deviation/7893736/

[5] AiS Watermark Pictures Protector. *Visible watermarking software* http://www.watermarker.com/

[6] uMark. Visible watermarking software, http://www.uconomix.com/

[7] WinsoftMagik. Visible watermarking software, http://www.winsoftmagic.com/

[8] HTML Image Splitter, http://html-image-splitter.forthtech-software.qarchive.org/

[9] CopyZero, http://www.costozero.org/wai/copyzero.html

[10] Digital signatues, http://en.wikipedia.org/wiki/Digital_signatures

[11] Cryptographyworld, public keys, http://www.cryptographyworld.com/what.htm

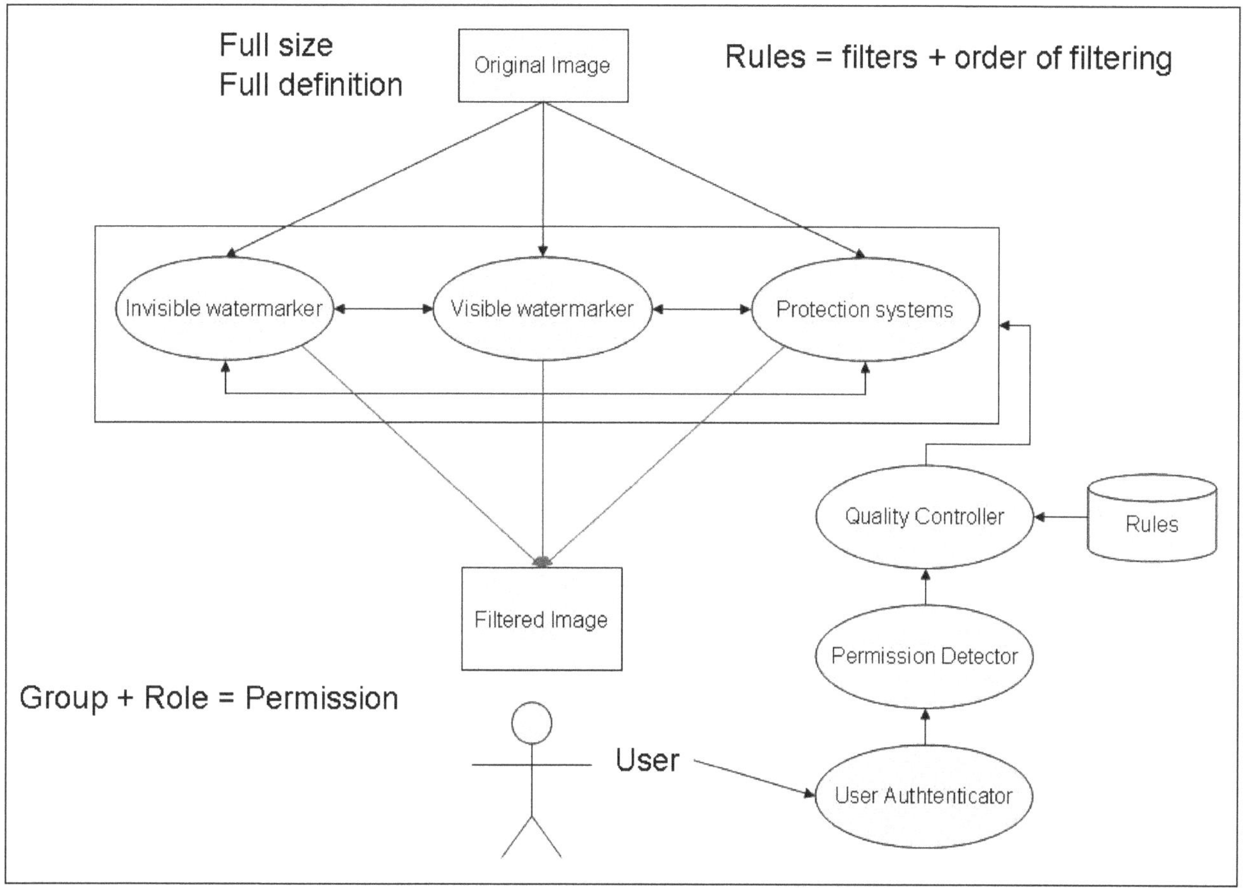

Fig. 8.10. Automatic Images Protection Architecture

WEBSITES AND INTELLECTUAL PROPERTY RIGHTS*

Giuliana DE FRANCESCO

Ministero per i Beni e le Attività Culturali, Direzione Generale per l'Innovazione Tecnologica, Osservatorio Tecnologico per i Beni e le Attività Culturali, Via Michelangelo Caetani, 32 00186 Roma, ITALY, E-mail: defrancesco@beniculturali.it

Ministry for Cultural Heritage and Activities, Directorate General for Technological Innovation and Promotion, Technology Observatory for Cultural Heritage and Activities (Ministero per i beni e le attività culturali. Direzione generale per l'innovazione tecnologica e la promozione. Osservatorio tecnologico per i beni e le attività culturali)

Abstract: *Before a website is designed and published, it is necessary to be aware of rights – especially intellectual property rights – inherent in material which is to be inserted and those which will pertain to the finished site. The term "intellectual property rights" was coined in the English-speaking world and unites industrial property and copyright law. Thus it specifies, on one hand, rights regarding brands and trademarks in general and patents for inventions and models (covered in Italy by industrial law) and, on the other, those statutes which protect the products of creative talent. These safeguards are organized in different systems in different countries; the two most common are the Roman-Germanic "droit d'auteur" and, in countries with common law, copyright. In the face of the recent increase in the protection accorded by the law to intellectual property, the field has undergone rapid development and grown in complexity, also as a result of various initiatives facilitating the wide circulation of material and free access to it.*
Keywords: *IPR, Copyright, Digitisation, Creative Commons*

Résumé: *Avant de procéder au projet et à la publication d'un site web il faut être informé des droits et avant tout des droits de propriété intellectuelle, qui existent sur le contenues à insérer, et de ceux que l'on acquerra une fois conclue l'œuvre. L'expression "droits de propriété intellectuelle" (intellectual property rights), forgé dans le milieu anglo-saxon, réuni le industrial property e la copyright law; elle indique donc d'un coté les droits relatifs à des labels et à des marques distinctives en général et aux brevets d'invention et des models, réglementés par nous dans le cadre du droit industriel, et de l'autre coté le droits d'auteur, c'est à dire l'ensemble des tutelles auxquelles les ouvrages de type créatif sont soumis. Ces tutelles s'organisent de façon différente selon les Pays; les deux systèmes les plus diffusés sont ceux de souche latino-germanique des droits d'auteur et du copyright, typique des pays de common law. En présence de la récente intensification de la protection accordée par la loi à la propriété intellectuelle, le panorama est enrichi et innové rapidement par les résultats des différentes initiatives qui se développent pour offrir des alternatives qui encouragent la circulation et le libre accès aux ouvrages.*
Mots cles: *IPR, Copyright, Numérisation, Creative Commons*

INTELLECTUAL PROPERTY RIGHTS[1]

Before undertaking the design and publishing of a website, it is necessary to be aware of the rights inherent in the material which is to be inserted and those which will pertain to the finished product.

The term "intellectual property rights" was coined in the English-speaking world and unites industrial property and copyright law. Thus it specifies, on one hand, rights regarding brands and trademarks in general and patents for inventions and models (industrial property) and, on the other, those statutes which protect the products of creative talent. These safeguards are organized in different systems in different countries; the two most common are the Roman-Germanic "author's rights" and, in countries with common law, copyright.

In the face of the recent increase in the protection accorded by the law to intellectual property, the field has undergone rapid development and grown in complexity also as a result of various (alternative) initiatives facilitating the wide circulation of material and free access to it.

Author's rights and copyright, the convergence between regulations, and new licensing procedures

The *droit d'auteur* system is based on the centrality of the author, owner of the moral rights regarding the creation and integrity of a work, which never expire and cannot be

* This paper is an adaptation of the article *Siti web e diritti di proprietà intellettuale*, published in the *Manuale per la qualità dei siti web pubblici e culturali* (© MINERVA 2005) pp. 177-194. A complete update of the reference list is unfortunately lacking. Among the fundamental references are: Sirotti Gaudenzi, A., Il nuovo diritto d'autore: la proprietà intellettuale nella società dell'informazione, 2003, Sant'Arcangelo di Romagna, Maggioli; Cunegatti, B.; Di Cocco, C.; Monducci, J., Immissione nel sito web della regione Emilia Romagna di materiale informativo coerentemente alla normativa in materia di proprietà intellettuale e trattamento dei dati personali: linee guida, 2003; De Robbio, A. (ed.) Diritto d'autore: la proprietà intellettuale tra biblioteche di carta e biblioteche digitali, 2001, Roma, AIB Sezione Lazio; De Robbio, A., Copyright elettronico per la Biblioteca digitale italiana, 2003, in: Studio di fattibilità per la realizzazione della biblioteca digitale, Aggiornamento 2002-2003, Intersistemi <http://www.iccu.sbn.it/PDF/aggSDF_pt-4.pdf>; European Museums Information Institute Distributed Content Framework – CORN, N. *et al.*, edd., EMII DCF Workpackage 2, Legal requirements report and licensing agreement templates, 2003, © EMII-DCF; MINERVA WP4. Italian Woking Group "Problems Connected to Data Protection and Intellectual Property Rights in Relation to On-line Accessibility of Cultural Heritage", Working paper "Data protection and intellectual property rights in relation to on line accessibility of cultural heritage. First remarks" Vers. 1.0 – 15 giugno 2004 (http://www.minervaeurope.org/structure/workinggroups/servprov/ipr/documents/wp4ipr040615firstremarks.pdf).

1 All URLs quoted in the paper were correct as of 7th March 2005.

transferred to others. This means that the author of a work must in all cases be credited using the form of identification he or she has chosen (right of "paternity"). In addition, the text must not be altered or abridged without the author's approval (right of integrity) and may not be published without the author's permission or – in the case of an unpublished work – published without the consent of the author's heirs or legatees. In no case may a work be published when this has been forbidden by the author (right to not publish).

The author's rights are inherent and require no formal assertion, such as the deposition or registration of the work, in order to exercised.

Together with these moral rights, the author or the author's heirs are entitled to the exclusive economic use of the work for a specified period of time; the general rule in Europe is currently seventy years after the author's death. The economic rights can be transferred from the author to a publisher or other persons (who may or may not be involved in the work's production and sale). Transmission of a work via Internet is considered to be an exclusive right of public distribution.

Exceptions may be made to an author's rights in cases of recognised public interest, namely limitations to these rights or the possibility of unrestricted use. In no circumstances do these exceptions allow the violation of moral rights or the economic exploitation of a work without the author's permission. It should be noted that certain exceptions to the law, such as with regard to photographic reproduction, cannot be automatically transferred to digitization, which has a different legal status.

In addition to the author's rights, what are known as connected rights – associated with the object of the author's rights – are recognised with respect to persons other than the author who performed auxiliary or mediatory roles during the production of the work. This category includes, for example, artists who interpret or perform (e.g. actors, singers, musicians and dancers), the producers of films and musical and audiovisual recordings, the rights associated with radio and television broadcasts, including review and scientific programmes, scenography sketches and photography.

Under the copyright system, found in countries with common law,[2] the moral rights are less clearly defined and an author may generally relinquish them, whilst attention is focused on the economic exploitation of a work.

In place of exceptions, copyright law makes reference to fair use, or fair dealing: for the purpose of study or research, or other socially useful activities, under certain conditions the use without previous authorization of parts of a work protected by copyright is permitted, as long as this does not constitute commercial exploitation of it. In countries with civil law where there is a system of authors' rights, the term *copyright* is often used; it is usually employed to indicate the economic or patrimonial rights forming part of the author's rights.[3]

Since a creative work is by its very nature made to circulate without respect for national boundaries and be re-used, there have been attempts since the 19th century to seek international agreement between the various national laws in force. The first important steps were taken at a convention in Paris for the protection of industrial property in 1883, most recently amended at Stockholm in 1967, and the Berne Convention on literary and artistic property (1886, revised up until 1971).[4] The latter established the principal of territoriality, which is still today the basis of international regulations concerning an author's rights: a work is protected by the laws of the country of use, regardless of the legislation in force in the author's land of origin or the author's nationality. Since 1988 various European Parliament and EEC directives have further increased the uniformity of authors' rights legislation in member countries of what is now the European Union.

These European directives have been progressively inserted into the various national laws of EU member states. Thus there now exist three levels of protection of authors' rights: international, European Union and national.[5]

[2] England, Wales and many countries that were once British colonies, including the USA (except for Louisiana), Australia and South Africa. As opposed to civil law, found in many continental European countries, which is rooted in Roman law.

[3] For more about these two systems, their similarities and differences: Pascuzzi, G.; Caso, R., I diritti sulle opere digitali: copyright statunitense e diritto d'autore italiano, 2002, Padova, CEDAM.

[4] In 1967, under the auspices of the UN, the World Intellectual Property Organization was founded (WIPO, < http://www.wipo.int>), heir and administrator of the Berne Convention and other international conventions. In 1996 the WIPO Copyright Treaty (WCT) and WIPO Performances and Phonograms Treaty (WPPT) were signed, both ratified by the EEC in 1996. A recent international agreement was TRIPS, Trade Related Aspects of Intellectual Property Rights, promoted by the WTO <http://www.wto.org>, which concerns all aspects of intellectual property rights with commercial implications, both authors' and industrial property rights.

[5] Numerous portals and virtual reference desks offer guidance and information about regulations. International examples are: About Intellectual Property (WIPO), <http://www.wipo.org/about-ip/en/>; Intellectual Property Gateway (WTO), < http://www.wto.org/english/tratop_e/trips_e/trips_e.htm>; Unesco Page on Copyright, <http://www.unesco.org/culture/copyright/> and Unesco Collection of Copyright Laws, <http://portal.unesco.org/culture/en/ev.php-URL_ID=14991&URL_DO=DO_TOPIC&URL_SECTION=-471.html>.
European sources: EUR-LEX: rights in the European Union. Intellectual property rights <http://europa.eu.int/eur-lex/it/lif/reg/it_register_1720.html>; Introduction to intellectual property, furnished by the European Union site ScadPlus, Mercato interno section (in Italian) <http://europa.eu.int/scadplus/leg/it/s06020.htm>; and (especially) the IPR-Helpdesk Web Service <http://www.ipr-helpdesk.org/index.htm>, a free service supporting creativity and innovation in Europe financed by the European Commission; inside, e-serial: IPR Helpdesk Bulletin <http://www.ipr-helpdesk.org/controlador.jsp?cuerpo=cuerpo&seccion=newsletter&len=it>.
Countries with common law can refer to: UK Copyright Service, <http://www.copyrightservice.co.uk/>; United States Copyright Office, <http://www.copyright.gov/>.

The introduction of IT has profoundly modified the setting in which creative works are produced and used. The arrival on the scene of the Internet, an exceptionally efficient means of communicating such works, has caused a notable acceleration in their circulation and created a confrontation between the plurality of legal formulations and the unity of the Web; this has stimulated an intensified international effort to negotiate legislative harmony. This process has seen the development of a marked international emphasis on the protection of intellectual property: in a society based on information and knowledge, intellectual property is clearly of fundamental importance. The regulatory scene is evolving rapidly and becoming more complex, and the penalties for transgression are increasing.

As a reaction against growing limitations, groups of authors have chosen to privilege the diffusion of their work and renounce, in part or totally, the economic rights offered by the law, so as to avoid the ever-increasing restrictions imposed on the circulation of works by regulations which protect authors' rights. The established practice has become the distribution of the work accompanied by a standard licence which may authorize some or all of the uses reserved by law.[6] Those who wish to offer their work to the public without imposing any conditions whatsoever may make it available in the public domain with "no rights reserved". Similar initiatives are often grouped under the label "copyleft".[7]

In the years of the new millennium a new concept entered the dialectic between the protection of authors' rights, and freedom of information and the free circulation of creative works, first in the USA – but with international extent – the Creative Commons initiative. It grew from the need to guarantee a free choice and control over circulation to authors, aiming to make immediately clear to every potential user the operations to which the author consents and which rights are reserved ("some rights reserved"). Creative Commons has proposed a set of standard licences which serve to regulate the various exclusive rights regarding economic use guaranteed by law to an author that follow a progressive series, intermediate with respect to traditional authors' rights (all rights reserved) and the public domain (no rights reserved).

These licences are made freely available to those who wish to make use of them; their duration is specified by the regulations protecting creative works and they may not be revoked, although the conditions may be overruled by agreements made directly with the author. Four criteria were used in drawing up the licences: *attribution*: recognition of the author's "paternity"; *non commercial use*: prohibition of use of the work in such a way as to make profits without the author's prior authorization; *no derivative works*: the work must be circulated in its original form, no alteration is permitted; *share alike*: all works produced using that distributed with the licence must be subject to the same conditions of use. The various possible combinations of these four elements yield the standard forms of the licence. Licences exist in three versions: *human readable (commons deed)*; *lawyer readable (legal code)*; *machine readable (digital code)*, designed (respectively) for normal users, lawyers and computers. The digital code can be readily copied and transferred to a website, thus making explicit those rights which the author retains and allowing search engines to select content on the basis of the adoption of standardized licences.

The Creative Commons site[8] offers guidance to the choice of the licence most appropriate for each specific need and provides the necessary technical information for their incorporation into web resources. It is thus a useful point of reference for those entitled to rights concerning material they put on websites, and who wish to make clear which uses they authorize and which they do not.

The International Commons (iCommons) Project aims to translate the licences and adapt them to diverse national legal systems. The University of Turin Law Department has adapted the Creative Commons licences for use in Italy. On 16th December 2004 the Italian Creative Commons licences were launched.[9]

In November 2004 the Science Commons Project commenced, with the aim of examining the possible application of Creative Commons licences to the world of academic science, so as to promote scientific innovation by facilitating the exchange of knowledge.[10]

OTHER REGULATIONS

In giving access to cultural material, attention must be given to other legislation which applies to aspects other than intellectual property rights. An important difference is that whereas (since the Berne Convention) authors' rights are protected in accordance with the law in the state

Italy: Pagina del diritto d'autore e del copyright, ed. Antonella De Robbio, <http://www.math.unipd.it/~derobbio/dd/copyr00.htm>; AIB page on Diritti d'autore, diritti all'informazione e biblioteche, <http://www.aib.it/aib/cen/copyright.htm>; highly informative and constantly updated: <www.dirittodautore.it>.

[6] For example the Gnu Free Documentation Licence – GFDL, <http://www.gnu.org/copyleft/fdl.html>. The best-known open content product is perhaps the collaborative web encyclopaedia Wikipedia <http://www.wikipedia.org>.

[7] A general introduction to copyleft is given by Marandola, M., Il nuovo diritto d'autore: introduzione a Copyleft, Open Access e Creative Commons, 2005, Milano, DeC.

[8] Website: <http://www.creativecommons.org>.

[9] Vedi <http://www.creativecommons.it/Licenze>. Several members of Creative Commons Italia have launched the "Scarichiamoli!" initiative <http://www.scarichiamoli.org/>, which aims to introduce a parliamentary bill prosing that all creative works whose production is financed by public funds should be in the public domain. The law would also facilitate the use of works in the public domain, obliging the state to establish a dedicated portal giving access to public domain works in the various fields of art and research.

[10] <http://science.creativecommons.org>

in which the work is used, regardless of the degree of protection offered by legislation in the country where the work was produced, with regard to other rights what is legal in one nation may be against the law and prejudicial to some legally-protected right in another. Internet crosses borders and territories with different cultures whose differing values are expressed in their legal systems.

Laws which define obscenity and indecency, for example, may vary considerably from place to place. Under some legal systems the publication of particular categories of material is subject to restrictions (for example the prohibition of spreading Nazi propaganda) or special protection, as in the case of photographs of children.

When giving Internet access to information concerning cultural heritage, relevant legislation must clearly be respected, and the risks to which unenclosed heritage sites might be subjected due to the spread of information should be born in mind.[11]

The question of the right to privacy deserves particular attention,[12] since its importance increases as does the provision of Internet services. In order to give remote access to the services offered by cultural institutions it is often necessary to process, more or less automatically, users' personal details. Especial care must be exercised to avoid the possibility that automatic resource administration and monitoring systems might fail to respect the right to privacy regarding personal information.

Prudence must be used in the management of community services. Whereas cultural institutions have begun to make use of the opportunities offered by the collaborative Web 2, most community services are limited to mailing lists. Although it is by now clearly established that forwarding a private e-mail without the author's knowledge constitutes a violation of the author's rights and the right to privacy, neither must list archives be made publicly accessible beyond the circle of participants; permission should always be obtained from those involved.

RIGHTS CONCERNING THE DESIGN AND CONSTRUCTION OF WEBSITES

In the early stages of designing the structure and contents of a site it is necessary to decide which material will be incorporated and to find out what rights pertain to it, identify the owners of these and (in all cases in which the right holders are not the person or body responsible for the website) obtain the necessary permission or licence. Disregard for the law involves the risk of legal action and the obligation of paying damages; violation of the author's moral rights is particularly serious (failure to acknowledge or usurpation of the work's authorship, modification causing offence to the author's reputation or honour, publication of a work not intended for publication). Even if we leave aside these considerations, those who behave incorrectly risk being discredited and compromising their relationship with authors and users.

Certain material, such as multimedia works and databases, may be associated with numerous rights and right holders, and tracing them will not be easy. In complex situations it is advisable to take specialist legal advice.

For every "creative work"[13] to which one wishes to give public access through a website, the following questions must be answered:

- Who is/are the author(s)? The author is held to be that indicated as such in the work itself, but this information may not be clearly and completely supplied in every work.
- Are exclusive rights to economic use still in force? Or has the author transferred them completely or partially, e.g. to a commercial editor, or renounced them completely or in part, e.g. using a Creative Commons licence?

The administration of rights pertaining to a work may have been delegated to a third party (in Italy, the society SIAE);[14] if the work bears no copyright declaration, a check could be made in the listings of such a company.

The next stage will be an evaluation of the way in which this selected material is to be used. Will it be published in its entirety or in part? On one or more web pages? Will it be modified or reworked? Lastly, an estimate must be

[11] Cf: MINERVA WP4. Italian Woking Group "Problems Connected to Data Protection and Intellectual Property Rights in Relation to On-line Accessibility of Cultural Heritage", Working paper "Data protection and intellectual property rights in relation to on line accessibility of cultural heritage. First remarks" (http://www.minervaeurope.org/structure/workinggroups/servprov/ipr/documents/wp4ipr040615firstremarks.pdf).

[12] The European Human Rights Convention (1950) established for the first time that each person has a right to personal and family privacy, also regarding their home and correspondence. In 1995 procedures were started to create uniformity between pertinent legislation in EU member countries, European Parliament and Government Directive 95/46/EC concerning the protection of individuals with regard to the treatment of personal information. The protection of privacy with respect to electronic communication is dealt with by Directive 2002/58/CE of the European Parliament and Government, 12th July 2002, concerning the processing of personal data and the protection of privacy in the electronic communications sector. In Italy, the question is covered by the personal data protection law (D. lgs. 30th June 2003, n. 196), and with an attachment concerning professional ethics and good practice in the handling of personal data for historical purposes.

[13] Italian authors' rights legislation protects "le opere dell'ingegno di carattere creativo che appartengono alla letteratura, alla musica, alle arti figurative, all'architettura, al teatro ed alla cinematografia, qualunque ne sia il modo o la forma di espressione. Sono altresì protetti i programmi per elaboratore come opere letterarie ai sensi della convenzione di Berna sulla protezione delle opere letterarie ed artistiche [...] nonché le banche di dati che per la scelta o la disposizione del materiale costituiscono una creazione intellettuale dell'autore". [art. 1].

[14] The Italian Society of Authors and Publishers, <http://www.siae.it>. In the "Biblioteca giuridica" section the site provides a collection of national, EU, international and Italian legal material on authors' rights. A useful international source is the International Federation of Reproduction Rights Organisations –IFRRO, <http://www.ifrro.org/>.

made of the intended time for which the work will be used. Then a permit or licence for its use may be requested.[15]

When planning the inclusion of material in a site it must be remembered that cutting and pasting, as well as reworking, translating or adapting a legally protected work require the prior acquisition of the author's permission.

Italian law allows the free circulation of:

- Texts of official documents produced by the state or other public bodies, Italian or otherwise, which are not protected by author's rights (art. 5 lda);[16]
- News articles of economic, political or religious nature, unless the use of these is expressly restricted. In all cases, the source, date and author's name must be indicated (art. 65 lda);
- If the same conditions (the obligation to indicate the source, correctly and completely) are respected, the texts of speeches of political or administrative interest made in conferences open to the public, and extracts from these, may be used (art. 66 lda);
- Extracts from works may be summarized or quoted for the purposes of information or criticism, as long as this does not constitute competition in the economic exploitation of the work and on the condition that the author, title and publisher are always cited (art. 70 lda);
- Works that are not original or creative in character, as long as these are not protected by law;
- Works whose period of legal protection regarding rights of ownership (exclusive rights to economic exploitation) has expired. The author's moral rights, which are not subject to limitation, must however be respected.

There follows an explanation of the rights that may pertain to several kinds of work which are frequently used in cultural websites.

Photographs and Static Images

In the case of Italian law, images produced using procedures similar to those employed in photography are included in the same category (art. 2 comma 7, art. 87), which would imply that digital photographs are protected in the same way as those which are chemically produced.

The first fundamental distinction that must be made, though problematic due to the lack of objective criteria for judgement, is between creative photography of artistic value and every-day photography ("images of people or aspects, elements or events of the natural world or social life", art. 87 lda). Cropping or superimposing other material on an artistic photograph without prior permission of the author would be a violation of the latter's moral rights. With respect to ordinary photographs, the photographer possesses an exclusive "connected" right to the reproduction, diffusion and sale of the photograph for twenty years from when it was taken; when the photograph was taken during the fulfilment of a contract of employment, the right belongs to the employer. In order that this right be exercised, the photograph must bear the photographer's name (or that of his or her employer or client), the year it was taken and the name of the author of any work which is reproduced. This information must therefore accompany every image which is published on a website. No protection is given to a third category of images: photographs of writing, documents, business papers, objects, technical drawings and suchlike, which are considered merely as records (art. 87-92 lda).

It is not, though, sufficient to cite a photograph, name the right holders and acquire the necessary permission for publication on the Web; consideration must also be given to the subject reproduced. For example:

- The portrait of a person cannot be circulated without his or her explicit consent, unless it is of a public figure or in the photograph of a ceremony or other public event (art. 96-98). A museum, for example, cannot publish on its site the image of a single visitor absorbed in the contemplation of an exhibit without the visitor's explicit permission.
- In the case of a photograph of a work of art, the rights of the author of which are still protected by law, the necessary permission must be obtained from the holder of ownership rights. If the exclusive rights to the economic use of a work have expired and the work has come under the state tutelage as part of the national cultural heritage, reproduction of the image must be authorized by the body responsible, which may fix fees and conditions. (Cultural Heritage and Landscape Law[17] art. 106-109, in particular art. 108).

Correspondence

The letters of historical or well-known figures are particularly fascinating; they provoke curiosity and it is easy to succumb to the temptation to exhibit them to the public. Private letters however cannot be made public without the explicit consent of both writer and recipient. In Italian law, these rights are connected to authors' rights and recognised for all private correspondence, be it protected or not by authors' rights, and remain valid after the expiry of these. This protection does not apply to

[15] Contract templates for the public communication of various types of material via Internet are proposed in Chimienti, L., Il diritto di autore nella prassi contrattuale, 2003, Milano, Giuffrè, pp. 295-350.

[16] A guide to documents available in the Italian public domain is available on the site of the Associazione italiana biblioteche, <http://www.aib.it/dfp/>

[17] D. lgs. 22nd January 2004, n. 42, in force since 1st May 2004.

official correspondence or when the national interest is at stake (art. 93-95 lda).

Databanks

Databanks,[18] known as databases when associated with a database management system, are protected as creative works if the choice or arrangement of the contents may be considered an original work of intellect (art. 1 lda). The author of a databank has the exclusive right to decide whether to approve any reproduction, distribution or public presentation, complete or partial, of the databank and any translation or adaptation (art. 64 quinquies lda).

In addition, the compiler of a databank of less than "creative" status is entitled to specific protection in European Union member countries, a type of right known as *sui generis*. This protects the investment represented by the construction and development against unfair competition or parasitic exploitation of a databank, prohibiting the extraction or re-use of its contents for fifteen years from the date of completion.

The rights pertaining to material which forms part of the databank are not affected; the software employed has also independent protection.

Graphics

The external elements of works are protected; the imitation is forbidden, as unfair practice, "of headings, emblems, embellishments, arrangements of signs or letters, any other detail of form or colour of the work's external appearance, when such reproduction or imitation could create confusion with regard to a work or its author" (art. 102 lda).

The original graphic work of a site merits protection as would any other artistic production; this does not preclude the drawing of inspiration from a well-produced piece of computer graphics, because illegality consists in imitation that creates confusion on the part of the user with respect to the imitated site.

Logos and Trademarks

It is not possible to consider here the field of industrial property, but it should be remembered that the law forbids the unauthorized use of logos and trademarks. A trademark may consist of a word or phrase; its function is to allow the identification of a commercial product (that might be, for example, a periodical) on the part of potential users. Registered or deposited trademarks are generally indicated by the letter R inside a circle ® or the acronym ™.

[18] The following definition of a databank is given (art. 2 comma 9 lda): "raccolta di opere, dati o altri elementi indipendenti sistematicamente o metodicamente disposti ed individualmente accessibili mediante mezzi elettronici o in altro modo".

Linking and Framing

Techniques which are commonly used in the creation of a site, linking, framing and inlining, also have legal implications.

The term *link* is used to indicate a hypertextual connection, a fundamental instrument for navigating the Web which allows a user consulting a particular web page to be directly connected to a different page, either within or external to the site. The expression *framing* refers to the insertion of a particular page into the graphics structure of the site that connects to it; *inlining* refers to the insertion in a site of images which reside physically in other sites.

Links within the same site pose no legal problems; the same applies to connections to the home pages of external sites (*surface linking*), which is generally welcomed and hoped for. Closer attention must be given to *framing* and what is known as *deep linking*, connecting directly to other sites' internal pages without passing through the home page.

Both practices are considered illegal in the USA if specific permission has not been given by the owner of the linked-to site. European and Italian legislation does not seem to have reached a unified common position: *framing* is held to violate an author's rights when the source of the information presented on the screen is not made explicit, and may be considered unfair practice when the fame of another site or the services it provides are exploited without authorization or payment.

The practice of *deep linking*, which has the effect of bypassing a site's home page – that generally features advertising banners and visitor-counting devices – could be considered a violation of regulations regarding competition. It is clear, on the other hand, that only indicating the full URL of a page or electronic resource, in every case a standard identifier is missing,[19] allows the digital resource to be unambiguously identified and contacted.

The sites of some organizations explain the *links policy* they use and that which they would like to see employed by those who wish to link to the site's internal pages, often requesting that prior contact be made with the webmaster to obtain permission.[20]

In making use of information from other sites, then, it is good practice to be prudent and correct at all times, keeping in mind the possible implications of our actions; on the other hand, in order to protect our material, it is advisable always to make clear how we would like others

[19] Such as *persistent identifiers*, the Digital Object Identifier (DOI), the Universal Resource Name (URN) etc.

[20] Good examples are the United Kingdom Museums, Archives and Libraries Council website, <http://www.mla.gov.uk> and the site of the Emilia Romagna regional administration, Italy.

to behave with respect to *deep links*, for example with an explanation in the copyright-disclaimer note (see below).

Software

Before using programmes for managing site material and for uploading it onto a server, it is necessary to be in possession of valid licences for their use. Computer programmes are protected in Europe by authors' rights laws, though with the exclusion of the ideas and principles on which a programme is based. Since 1991 it has been European Union policy to try and create uniformity in this field of legislation.[21]

Since the 1980s the free software movement has been actively supporting the collaborative development and free distribution of programmes which may shared and modified. Evolution in this area has lead to *open source* software, which is distributed with a licence which consents access to the source code and which may therefore be freely shared, copied and modified, on the usual condition that use of the derived programme be subject to the same conditions.[22] European public authorities increasingly encourage the adoption of open source software as part of a policy of cooperation, transferability and interoperability, and also because a programme which many experts from different backgrounds may correct and improve promises to perform better and give results of higher quality.[23]

Domain Name, Meta Tag

When defining a domain name the laws which protect copyright must be respected, and also those regarding names, distinctive signs and trademarks.[24]

When giving a name to a site, it must be born in mind that legal protection also covers a creative work's title, which, "when it specifies the work itself, may not be reproduced on another work without the author's permission" (art. 100 lda). Care must therefore be taken not to use for one's site the title of a work protected by law, in the same way as attention is needed for the names of organizations or products, or those registered as trademarks or signs, and therefore protected by the laws covering industrial property.

Similar considerations apply to headings and the key words used for indexing in the *meta tags* in page headers, which contain the information needed for a search engine to find the site.

SITE PROTECTION

A website, once it is constructed with full regard for the rights inherent in the material it contains, may itself be considered an original or creative work, and thus subject to legal protection, without in any way prejudicing the rights pertaining to its contents. In order to understand the degree of legal protection to which a site is entitled, it necessary to analyse the characteristics of the work which the site represents and verify whether this may be considered an original, creative work.

Since a site is generally composed of an interconnection of different types of work (texts, images, sounds and graphics), only exists in digital form, requires software for its construction and use, and is generally interactive in nature, the prevalent tendency is to consider it a form of multimedia work.

A multimedia work may in turn be defined as a collective work, made up of a "number of whole or partial works which together constitute an autonomous creation, as a result of choice and coordination so as to achieve a particular end" (art. 3 lda), in which case the author may be considered the assembler (art. 38 lda). Alternatively, it may be considered a complex (group) work, the result of the indistinguishable and indivisible contributions of more than one person, in which case the author's rights belong to all of the co-authors together (art. 10 lda).

The appropriate form of protection must be determined for each single case according to the nature of the website.

Copyright Notice and Disclaimer

Creative works are protected by inherent authors' rights, which require no particular formalities: such a website is thus subject to legal protection for the mere fact of its having been created. It is, however, advisable to make explicit that one intends to reserve one's rights with regard to a site which has been placed online by means of a *copyright notice*, so as to deter theft and plagiarism, give clear indications to those who act in good faith, and provide those who wish to request authorization for the use of a part of the contents with the information they need.

The simplest, clearest and most widely used form of *copyright notice* is "All rights reserved", but it is also possible to list in detail those rights which are reserved and uses of the material which are forbidden, for example a prohibition to create mirror versions of the site or download, re-transmit or modify files. The copyright

---

[21] Directive 91/250/CEE of the European Community Government (14th May 1991) on the legal protection of computer programmes, Italian D. lgs. 29th December 1992, n. 518.

[22] The site of the Open Source Initiative provides further information on the campaign and open source licences, <http://www.opensource.org>.

[23] The European Commission IDABC (Interoperable Delivery of European eGovernment Services to public Administrations, Business and Citizens) <http://europa.eu.int/idabc/> has created an Open Source Observatory, <http://europa.eu.int/idabc/en/chapter/452>. In Italy, the Ministry for Innovation and Technology issued Directive 19th December 2003 Sviluppo ed utilizzazione dei programmi informatici da parte delle pubbliche amministrazioni (published in the G.U. n. 31 on 7th February 2004) which encourages public authorities to adopt open source software.

[24] See A. Sirotti Gaudenzi, Il nuovo diritto d'autore cit., pp. 225-240.

notice should be accompanied by the name of the copyright holder; it is also opportune to include the date of the site's web publication. If updates are made, the date may be expressed as the period between the two extremes of publication and the latest update (e.g. 2002-2005): the publication date is important in the case of an intellectual property rights dispute concerning the work.

If one intends to renounce one's rights, partially or totally, and consent to some kinds of use or any use in certain circumstances, it is necessary to state this in the copyright notice; it is important to be clear, exhaustive and brief, with correct legal references. It is also possible to make use of the standardized "some rights reserved" Creative Commons licences described above.

Copyright notices are often accompanied by *disclaimer* clauses; these should be included in all cases when one wishes to explicitly decline responsibility for any consequences to users which may result from the use of information provided by the site.

When deciding where to place the copyright notice and disclaimer it should be remembered that the function of these is to make clear to anyone who visits the site the situation regarding the legal rights to which they refer: irrespective of the graphics layout, these should be present on or accessible from each page.[25]

Technological Measures of Protection

The explanation in a website copyright notice of which types of use are permitted and which forbidden should prevent improper use by those who are in good faith.

There exist other, technological measures of protection for online digital resources, which range from the simple expedient of publishing images of low resolution, which limits their commercial usefulness, to digital watermarking, the (visible or invisible) insertion of the name of the owning institution and other information useful for electronic marking, encryption, and the various systems which allow material to be visualized but not downloaded.

These technological protective measures are important not only with regard to copyright protection, but also for the guarantee they afford to site contents with respect to tutelage of identity, integrity and authenticity.

The most recent European directive[26] incorporated into Italian law has introduced the prohibition to violate technological measures of protection, recognising at the same time that disabled persons must not be disadvantaged; in their interests all technological protection must be deactivated. There exist technological systems for the digital management of rights in a complex environment, which also allow electronic commerce (eCommerce) to function; these are collectively known as digital rights management systems, or DRMS.[27] DRMS are generally adopted in complex situations, in particular in cases in which third parties intervene between holders of rights and final users, and have notable costs. The necessary conditions for the development and implementation of DRMS are the identification of rights pertaining to the resources which the system will administer, the description of these by means of metadata present on each digital resource and the definition of rules according to which the system will function. The rules which regulate the situation are strictly dependent upon the context in which the system will operate and may include the division of users into classes, each of which differs with respect to obligations and privileges. In order to function, digital rights management systems need to deal with personal information regarding users that allows them to be authenticated; during their development, selection and implementation therefore, legislation regarding the treatment of personal data must be taken into consideration.[28]

---

[25] Further suggestions may be found at: UK Copyright Service, Factsheet No. P-03: Copyright Notices, <http://www.copyrightservice.co.uk/copyright/p03_copyright_notices> (but note that some suggestions refer to the Anglo-American copyright model)

[26] Directive 2001/29/CE of the European Parliament and Government (22nd May 2001) on the harmonisation of certain aspects of copyright and related rights in the information society, Italian D. lgs. 9th April 2003, n. 68

[27] "DRM must be about the 'digital management of rights' not the 'management of digital rights", W3C Workshop on Digital Rights Management on the Web, 22nd-23rd January 2001, <http://www.w3.org/2000/12/drm-ws/workshop-report.html>

[28] A brief presentation of the features of DRMS and the MINERVA Project's point of view may be found in the Working Paper of the Italian WP4 IPR Data protection and ipr cit.

A fuller treatment is provided by the Relazione informativa Digital Rights Management [October 2004], on the Ministry for Innovation and Technology site, < http://www.innovazione.gov.it/ita/normativa/pubblicazioni/digital_rights_management.shtml >.

The relationship between DRM and interoperability is discussed in the Final Report of the High Level Group on Digital Rights Management (March-July 2004). The group was founded by the European Commission in the context of the implementation of the Action Plan eEurope 2005; representatives of all components of digital contents production processes participated: organizations of content providers, authors and rights holders, publishers and telephone operators, equipment manufacturers, DRM developers, researchers and consumers' associations.

The European Bureau of Library, Information and Documentation Associations, <http://www.eblida.org> has discussed DRMS in the EBLIDA Position on digital rights management systems (February 2003) <http://www.eblida.org/position/index.htm> and replied to the document produced by the High Level Group on DRMS with Response to the European Commission consultation on the Final Report of the High Level Group on Digital Rights Management, March-July 2004, <http://www.eblida.org/position/HLGDRM_FinalReport_May-July04.htm>

www.ingramcontent.com/pod-product-compliance
Lightning Source LLC
LaVergne TN
LVHW070533110826
845147LV00017BA/983

9781407305301